Every Day with *Jesus*

MAY

Waverley Abbey Resources is a trading name of CWR: CWR, Waverley Abbey House, Waverley Lane, Farnham, Surrey GU9 8EP, UK Tel: 01252 784700

Email: mail@waverleyabbey.org Registered Charity No. 294387. Registered Limited Company No. 1990308.

Cover image: iStock

Printed in the UK by Yeomans

WAVERLEY ABBEY
RESOURCES

MIX
Paper from
responsible sources
FSC® C015900

Every Day with Jesus is available in large print from Waverley Abbey Resources. It is also available on **audio** and **DAISY** in the UK and Eire for the sole use of those with a visual impairment worse than N12, or who are registered blind. For details please contact **Torch Trust for the Blind**, Tel: 01858 438260. Torch House, Torch Way, Northampton Road, Market Harborough LE16 9HL.

Psalm 145:1–8

'One generation commends your works to another; they tell of your mighty acts. They speak of the glorious splendour of your majesty – and I will meditate on your wonderful works.' (vv4–5)

Passing through turbulent financial waters can make the present uncomfortable; the future uncertain. Yet, I refuse to nurse and rehearse anxiety. I choose faith over fear and despondency. Life may trigger a 'counsel of despair', but wisdom says, 'Wait on the Lord.'

Waiting is tiring. In ministry with Youth for Christ money was in short supply. We were called to live by faith, or what some cynics call 'dying by faith'. Whilst I found this exhausting, it was also exhilarating. With little financial security, my wife and I prayed on our knees daily, holding up a bill to ask for God's intervention. We never spoke of our needs or wrote prayer letters with hints. This was between us and God; God's school of faith development.

God came through, though we learnt once one bill was paid another swiftly followed. We had no savings and we muddled on. Life was exhausting. Today I wonder if it was exhausting because we failed to discern between our material desires and God's purpose. The former offers fantasy provision for our imagined needs. It's about protecting ourselves against scarcity. Yet, scarcity can act as God's crucible of faith. As the philosopher Claude Tresmontant stated, 'God asked the prophets to believe him because he affected verifiable demonstrations of all that he said.'

RELATED SCRIPTURE TO CONSIDER: Isa. 30:15–26; Heb. 11:1–16; Deut. 31:1–8; Micah 7:8–13; Heb. 13:1–10.

AN ACTION TO TAKE: Consider how you decide between desire and necessity in a way that produces righteousness?

A PRAYER TO MAKE: 'Lord, in repentance and rest is my salvation, in quietness and trust is my strength. Amen.' (Based on Isa. 30:15.)

Psalm 145:9–21

'The LORD watches over all who love him, but all the wicked he will destroy. My mouth will speak in praise of the LORD. Let every creature praise his holy name for ever and ever.' (vv20–21)

The promise that God watches over us is a great assurance for our faith. Having faith is to place complete confidence in an unseen, often unrealised promise. (Unrealised in as far as our circumstances are concerned.)

Indeed the reality of our faith is measured by the degree to which we will open our mouth in praise of God despite our disappointments and difficulties. I have on more than one occasion had to profess confidence in Him by an act of my will ahead of the feelings that overwhelm my senses.

Perhaps the purest measure of faith is when I have no external basis upon which to base such faith, yet I choose to do so anyway. I've learnt that as a parent – whilst I've been unable to prevent my daughter experiencing pain and heartache yet I've remained steadfast in my love and commitment towards her. Some things she can only learn through personal life experience.

She knows that I'm always present, even when distant. For love endures through all adversity and, whilst itself not an all sufficient answer to life's woes, offers a haven for safety and sustenance in every challenge we endure. Love, indeed, never fails!

RELATED SCRIPTURE TO CONSIDER: 1 Cor. 13:1–13; Rom. 8:18–39; 1 Chron. 16:8–36; Jer. 31:1–6.

AN ACTION TO TAKE: First identify and then give thanks to God for three things from yesterday.

A PRAYER TO MAKE: 'Lord, Your love is boundless and I take refuge within Your faithfulness. Amen.'

Write to **micha@edwj.org** and I'll write back personally and in confidence as soon as I can.

God's Word

2 Timothy 3:10–17

'All Scripture is God-breathed and is useful for teaching, rebuking, correcting and training in righteousness, so that the servant of God may be thoroughly equipped for every good work.' (vv16–17)

I'm grateful for the emails I've received from *Every Day with Jesus* readers. One change I'm delighted to implement is additional scriptures so we can pursue further study related to our daily reading.

The joy of Scripture is that it is the Word of God. Jesus, God's Word, is embedded in every verse of Scripture. The first disciples uncovered the New Testament truths from within the pages of the Old Testament from the prophets who faithfully recorded all God revealed to them and finally revealed in the incarnate Christ. The Gospel writers found their testimony mirrored throughout the Old Testament.

We are used to navigating Scripture by chapter and verse, but these are not God-inspired. Chapters were first added in the thirteenth century, with verses completed in the sixteenth, for our convenience.

Scripture reveals God's truth in each and every part – be it a chapter or just a few words. In our staff prayers at Waverley Abbey Trust I was struck by the first two words from a passage someone shared: 'After this...' I never heard what else was said, because I found God speaking to me from these two words for several weeks. To read Scripture is to encounter God. There are many ways of using it. So long as these lead to lives devoted to and revealing the life of God then the Word has done its work.

RELATED SCRIPTURE TO CONSIDER: Rom. 15:1–6; Isa. 55:10–11; Heb. 4:12–16; Prov. 4.

AN ACTION TO TAKE: Take up the challenge of learning more from God's Word through looking at 60 key turning points covered in *Bible 60*.
Visit **edwj.org/mj21-3may**

A PRAYER TO MAKE: 'Lord, help me to find You within Your Word and to live my life according to Your Word. Amen.'

WAVERLEY ABBEY TRUST

COLLEGE

RESOURCES

HOUSE

verleyabbeycollege.ac.uk   waverleyabbeyresources.org   waverleyabbeyhouse.org

Waverley Abbey Trust

We are a charity serving Christians around the world with practical resources and teaching. We support you to grow in your Christian faith, understand the times in which we live, and serve God in every sphere of life.

The five main areas we focus on are:

- **Bible Engagement**
- **Prayer**
- **Mental Wellbeing**
- **Leadership**
- **Spiritual Formation**

waverleyabbey.org

Listen Up!

Hebrews 2:1–9

'We must pay the most careful attention, therefore, to what we have heard, so that we do not drift away.' (v1)

The Bible is not one book, but a library of books. It has two testaments; the first, known as the Old Testament, records the laws, history and prophecies that preceded and foretold the ministry of Jesus. The second, known as the New Testament, reveals the life and teaching of Jesus, His passion, and the emergence of the Church made up of His disciples.

In those early years following Christ's Ascension, the first disciples recorded the narrative of Jesus' life and mission through the guidance of the Holy Spirit. As the devil sought to oppose the Christians, so instruction was needed to enable God's followers to know how they were to live.

When I became a Christian aged 19, from a completely unchurched background, I was introduced to the Bible and began a journey of discovering the truth about God and myself. It was in reading and praying through Scripture that I grew to know God as my friend and faced up to the challenges that following Christ presented me.

These placed demands on my choices and the direction for my life.

I was always free to say no to what God revealed, since Christian discipleship is always a process of personal decision taking. No-one can be forced to become, or live as, a Christian. It is the Bible that alone, as God's Word, can and will reveal God's way to anyone who chooses to follow Him.

RELATED SCRIPTURE TO CONSIDER: Isa. 40:1–11; Isa. 55:6–9; James 1:19–27; John 5:36–47.

AN ACTION TO TAKE: Note down the things that stand out to you from your Bible reading. What is God saying to you through them?

A PRAYER TO MAKE: 'Lord, I choose to listen and invite You to change me through the reading of Your Word. Amen.'

Commissioned

Matthew 28:11–20

'Therefore go and make disciples of all nations, baptising them in the name of the Father and of the Son and of the Holy Spirit, and teaching them to obey everything I have commanded you. And surely I am with you always, to the very end of the age.' (vv19–20)

Scripture is God's complete and final Word for His disciples. Jesus' final instruction to his disciples was to make Christian disciples who follow Jesus' teachings; God's way of life. To help us He left three tremendous gifts: His Word, His Spirit and each other.

His Word was already embedded throughout the Old Testament and then set out in the New Testament, guided by the Holy Spirit, the third person of the Trinity, who is God. This is why we turn daily to God's Word for wisdom and guidance. This same Spirit is the one who guides us as we read God's Word. We become increasingly familiar with the Holy Spirit, who leads us into all truth: 'But when he, the Spirit of truth, comes, he will guide you into all the truth. He will not speak on his own; he will speak only what he hears, and he will tell you what is yet to come' (John 16:13).

Finally, God gave us each other as the Church to learn together, encourage and support each other throughout life's many challenges. We're not designed to be alone, as God made clear at our creation.

I've spent over forty five years learning from God's Word, instructed by God's Spirit whilst encouraged by God's Church. This is the disciple's path.

RELATED SCRIPTURE TO CONSIDER: Gen. 2:15–25; Psa.119:9–16; 1 John 2:15–29; Heb. 12:1–12.

AN ACTION TO TAKE: Learn from God's Word, listen to God's Spirit and join with God's people to grow in faith.

A PRAYER TO MAKE: 'Lord, I desire to do Your will. Place Your law within my heart, guide me by Your Spirit and encourage me through Your Church. Amen.'

Romans 15:1–7

'For everything that was written in the past was written to teach us, so that through the endurance taught in the Scriptures and the encouragement they provide we might have hope.' (v4)

Hope gives us a sense of expectation. It grows from a root of trust. Approaching Scripture, I anticipate finding something fresh in my friendship with God. For it's a treasury of blessing and encouragement for all seeking instruction in making sense of and fully appreciating life.

We've already noted the Bible is a library of books – sixty-six to be exact. These books are not all the same; we have God's laws for life, poetry, history, and prophecy. The opening book, Genesis, deals with the purpose of life from its origins, whilst the final book, Revelation, addresses the end of time itself.

Whilst all of Scripture is inspired, both for our instruction and spiritual formation, we find it presented in a variety of forms. I remember my first wife Katey returning from a training weekend with Trevor Partridge and excited at the idea of copying key verses from the psalms and placing them prominently around the house. Each day, whether brushing her teeth or packing her bag, she recited the verses and allowed them to become a part of her life. A very different approach to my academic method. Yet, we each grew in our faithfulness and love of God.

We're invited to find our way to engage with Scripture to learn to live every day with Jesus. This will take time and exploration on our part.

RELATED SCRIPTURE TO CONSIDER: Josh. 1:1–9; Psa. 119:97–104; Luke 24:13–49; 2 Thess. 2:13–17.

AN ACTION TO TAKE: For an excellent overview of Scripture, read David Pawson's *Unlocking the Bible*.

A PRAYER TO MAKE: 'Lord, help me discover my best approach to Scripture so that I might daily deepen my friendship with You and learn to live every day with Jesus. Amen.'

Psalm 19

**'The law of the LORD is perfect, refreshing the soul.
The statutes of the LORD are trustworthy, making wise
the simple.'** (v7)

F our key benefits for our enrichment and development as God's
friends are acquired by reading Scripture.

First, Scripture refreshes the soul, that essential, immortal, part of us. The soul is that aspect that wonders about life's meaning, whilst yearning for purpose and destiny. Unsettling, it stirred me to explore answers in my quest for meaning for life, which I found in Christ Jesus.

Second, God's rules for life can be trusted. They challenge contemporary cultural assumptions, yet offer the only trustworthy path to a fulfilling life. Gladly they are very simple and easily grasped. Christianity is a simple faith for simple folk.

Third, despondency (which many of us experience and can quickly be dragged down into a pit of despair by) is addressed in God's Word, which offers assurance when facing difficulties. I've often disappointed myself with my failure to seize hold of God's promises, choosing instead to indulge in despair often born of self-pity. Only by returning to God's Word can I quietly emerge from my 'blue mood'.

Finally, without clear instruction, we're blind to life's pitfalls. God's Word offers a lamp to guide us on our way. It alone ensures we keep our eyes focussed on the purpose for which we are created and our ultimate destiny, eternal fellowship with God. God's Word is for our perpetual benefit.

RELATED SCRIPTURE TO CONSIDER: Psalm 19:9–14; Proverbs 10; Hebrews 1:1–4; Matthew 5:1–12.

AN ACTION TO TAKE: When reading Scripture, keep a note (I use an online journal app, Evernote) of the words that challenge your behaviour. Then reflect upon these and think about how you might make them part of your daily life in practice.

A PRAYER TO MAKE: 'Lord, refresh me daily through Your Word and open my eyes to the truth about myself and Your simple way of life. Amen.'

Psalm 1

'Blessed is the one who does not walk in step with the wicked or stand in the way that sinners take or sit in the company of mockers but whose delight is in the law of the LORD, and who meditates on his law day and night.' (vv1–2)

When I competed as a cross country runner, there were a number of well-known songs that I would play in my head to manage my pace. These enabled me to ensure that I competed effectively, whilst giving me confidence no matter the opposition.

Scripture is like that. We want to engage with it daily so that it becomes the refrain around which we organise all of life. Today, when I meet situations, a familiar scripture will spring to mind that helps and comforts me. I may not immediately know chapter and verse, yet I do recall and rest in God's truth.

One thing's certain: we will frequently be distracted by the busyness and demands of contemporary life. All too quickly such distractions cause us to deviate from God's way that's always rooted in Scripture. Which is why it's important to remember that God's Word is our guidebook for life. We have choices to make and my intention is only as good as the action I choose to take.

Day and night we are encouraged to meditate on and to be preoccupied with Scripture. This will only happen once we make a plan to spend time with Scripture. These Bible reading notes open a window into the Bible. The question is: will you climb through and explore the Bible more fully for yourself and choose to live by its precepts? Life is a marathon, not a sprint.

RELATED SCRIPTURE TO CONSIDER: Psa. 119:105–112; Psa. 1:1–6; Matt. 7:1–20; 1 Pet. 5:6–11.

AN ACTION TO TAKE: To increase your enjoyment and understanding of the Bible, take a look at Waverley Abbey Resource's *Cover to Cover* range: **edwj.org/mj21-8may**

A PRAYER TO MAKE: 'Lord, help me to make the time to sit with Your Word, to learn from You and so live effectively for You. Amen.'

New book for women from Jen Baker

An extract from the introduction of Jen Baker's latest book

One of the most profound truths in the Bible is that regardless of how we came into this world – whether by love, passion or violence – we were chosen. God is intentional and at the moment of creation you were not only His first choice, but His best choice. At birth, He knew the number of hairs on your head (or lack thereof) and the number of days before you. God is responsible for bringing us into the world, but what we do with that time – and the legacy we choose to leave – is solely our responsibility.

Choice was created at the birth of Creation. The first Hebrew word of the Bible means 'in the beginning' and the second means God (Elohim), with the third word, bara, meaning 'created'. Any type of creation, whether we are creating a meal or a memory, involves choice. Therefore, Elohim chose, before time was established, to express His love by appointing mankind as the recipient of His love; because love without an object to love is unfulfilled, empty and void of purpose. In other words, you are God's desire!...

My prayer is that as you read, fear will lose its grip, faith will come alive, and purpose will be realigned... positioning you for a lifetime of relentless, kingdom pursuit.

This is your time, and this is your choice – make it an unwavering one.

John 1:1–5

In the beginning was the Word, and the Word was with God, and the Word was God. (v1)

We have taken a week to consider God's Word. It is a living Word for it is Jesus we hold when we handle Scripture. The Bible is called God's Word and this is how Jesus is described. From before the foundation of the earth, God's Word existed. That same Word is available to us every day as we open and read Scripture.

Just as the Word is forever with God, so we engage with the presence of God when we choose to engage with Scripture. This has nothing to do with neither the condition in which we approach God's Word, nor the feelings we experience. For the Word is itself truth, regardless of how and where I find myself, my feelings or status.

It is the Word that alone can sustain the light of God in us in the face of apparently impossible odds, for darkness can never extinguish this light. There are experiences through which I have only been able to cling to God's Word by sheer force of will, for the darkness appeared all consuming. Yet today, the light of Christ remains alive within me – it is by faith alone that we are secure in Christ.

We always retain the freedom to take up, or set down God's Word; yet without it we will be blind to the presence of God in our life and His true purpose.

It is God's Word alone that nourishes and nurtures my life with Jesus. Today, and every day!

RELATED SCRIPTURE TO CONSIDER: Psa. 119:89–96; John 1:6–18; Heb. 10:19–39; Luke 8:4–15.

AN ACTION TO TAKE: Make an agreement between yourself and God to spend time with Scripture each day. To start, use 'Related Scripture to consider', fifteen minutes for reading and reflection.

A PRAYER TO MAKE: 'Word of God, light of the world, thank You that darkness can never overcome me whilst I hold on to You. Amen.'

Conversion

Jeremiah 33:1–3

'Call to me and I will answer you and tell you great and unsearchable things you do not know.' (v3)

Revival has drawn me for many years. I first met its reality when converted to Christianity. From an unchurched, cynical and critical background, I perceived Christianity as a refuge for the weak and vulnerable. But God intervened.

At University I one day found myself in church responding to an invitation to receive Christ. I was certainly interested in all I'd heard, but not entirely convinced.

However, I liked the down-to-earth preacher, Cuthbert Bardsley, then Bishop of Coventry. Chatting after the service, something rang true as he handed us all a Gospel. 'Tomorrow morning you'll wake up and your first thought will be, "Oh, no! What an idiot I've been." However, if you'll get out of bed, sit down, open this book anywhere and start reading, God will confirm you've made the best decision of your life'

Monday dawned, I woke and thought, 'Crikey, I'm an idiot. I've been duped by Christians.' Having liked Cuthbert, I reluctantly followed his advice and on a brisk October morning, and as I read this Gospel I knew that I had found God and God had found me. It was an experience I have never been able to deny or renounce, even when life circumstances have driven me to that point in pain filled with desperation.

As we noted last week: Jesus is in God's Word, the Bible. There I met Him and I was brought from death to life, the very meaning of revival.

RELATED SCRIPTURE TO CONSIDER: Psa. 85; Ezek. 36:16–38; John 3:1–21; Rom. 10:14–21.

AN ACTION TO TAKE: Consider what convinces you God is alive and keeps the flame of faith burning in your heart.

A PRAYER TO MAKE: 'Lord, thank You for Your word of life that revives me each and every day. Amen.'

God's extraordinary work

Jeremiah 33:6–11
'I will bring Judah and Israel back from captivity and will rebuild them as they were before.' (v7)

God always reveals purpose through His activity. For some, revival is an end in itself. Hence the volume of literature detailing past revivals. Today we also find that there are many attempts to replicate past reawakenings as recorded in historical narratives.

Wonderfully, God is the source of all creation and so creativity, fresh expressions of His presence, are never in short supply. What, I ask myself, might a work of revival look like today?

Certainly it would call us back to behaving as we were originally created to live. There would be the cleansing of the burden of sin, as well as a shift in its destructive effects across society. Much like when a toxic spill is cleaned and the damaged environment restored to its natural state. Our natural state is to be in friendship with God and living lives of obedience through prayer.

Remarkably, there is no rebellion that can destroy God's plan of salvation presented through Jesus. I've discovered that God will always bring us back from the brink should we choose to return. His action is always rooted in humanity's desires and the choices they make.

Revival is God's extraordinary work most certainly; yet, revival has its roots in the desires and choices I, and my Christian sisters and brothers, make. These reach well beyond the walls of the Church.

RELATED SCRIPTURE TO CONSIDER: Exod. 15:22–27; Gen. 17; Isa. 46:8–13; Rom. 12:1–8.

AN ACTION TO TAKE: If some distance has grown between you and God, take the decision to close it, because when we confess our sins God faithfully forgives and restores us.

A PRAYER TO MAKE: 'Lord, may I keep short accounts with You and ensure I live close to You each and every day. Amen.'

Write to **micha@edwj.org** and I'll write back personally and in confidence as soon as I can.

Acts 1:1–8

'But you will receive power when the Holy Spirit comes on you; and you will be my witnesses in Jerusalem, and in all Judea and Samaria, and to the ends of the earth.' (v8)

I consistently need to remind myself that I live to love and serve God. I'm too easily consumed by the moment, my aspirations and desires. Yet, I'll never find fulfilment and self-realisation outside of Jesus, and God's purpose for my life. My primary point of encounter with God is in prayer, reflecting on all God says through His Word.

Tomorrow is Ascension day, marking Jesus' return to His Father. Here He stands and intercedes for us. Too often I become engrossed in life's inessentials. But my one sure and certain hope, common to all the Church, is that Christ is risen.

However, we too require the power of God that those first disciples who turned the world upside down (or right side up) experienced. The Holy Spirit was poured out on those frightened disciples nine days after the Ascension. No longer were they left alone to imagine their next steps. They were anointed to live lives devoted to Christ and the social, economic and psychological benefits available to society once Christ is exalted at its heart.

This is a message we all too easily compromise, seeking peace with our world. But instead, we are invited to make our peace with God and reveal the way to fullness of life. As we join the disciples waiting for a fresh outpouring of the Spirit, let's once more pray we become witnesses to God's power and presence in all society.

RELATED SCRIPTURE TO CONSIDER: Psa. 2; Rom. 8:18–39; Heb. 6:1–12; Acts 2:42–47.

AN ACTION TO TAKE: Can we conceive the Church leading the world? Yet, without the Church living the gospel, society unravels and engages in perpetual civil war. Choose to live as Jesus commands, and so turn our world right side up!

A PRAYER TO MAKE: 'Lord, I choose to stand together with others and pray for Your will to be done on earth as it is in heaven over the nine days from Ascension to Pentecost. Amen.'

Acts 1:9–14

'After he said this, he was taken up before their very eyes, and a cloud hid him from their sight.' (v9)

After Jesus left, the disciples returned to Jerusalem to await the promised Spirit. They joined in continuous prayer for nine days from the Ascension to Pentecost. We know it was nine days because the Ascension happened forty days after the Resurrection, and Pentecost was celebrated fifty days after the Passover. The Resurrection was the day after Passover, so – 50 minus 40 minus 1 equals 9. For nine days, starting the day after Jesus' Ascension, the fledgling Church faithfully prayed for power from on high that they might fulfil Jesus' command to witness to the whole world. They faithfully waited as the angels commanded.

Waverley Abbey Trust invites you to join us and commit to pray for nine consecutive days, beginning tomorrow, for God's purposes in the world. Scripture is clear that when God's people agree together in prayer, His will emerges on the earth. The only prayer Jesus taught, the Lord's Prayer, instructs us to pray in this way.

As we pray together we will, with one united voice, pray for the same objective. Every day as we say 'Amen' at the conclusion of our prayer, it will be both amplified and multiplied many thousands of times around the world.

We also pray that all involved, having dedicated ourselves to prayer over these next nine days, will experience a fresh visitation of the Holy Spirit and become more engaged in worship and service of our God, just like those first disciples.

RELATED SCRIPTURE TO CONSIDER: Joel 2:1–5 & 25–32; Acts 1; Matt. 18:18–20.

AN ACTION TO TAKE: Consider getting to know the person and power of the Holy Spirit and enjoy a closer communion with Him.
Visit **edwj.org/mj21-13may**

A PRAYER TO MAKE: 'Lord, fill me with Your Holy Spirit daily so I can live the gospel for the benefit of all. Amen.'

Perseverance   FRIDAY 14 MAY

Daniel 1:1–17
'But Daniel resolved not to defile himself with the royal food and wine, and he asked the chief official for permission not to defile himself in this way.' (v8)

Discovering I couldn't have my own children was devastating. It drove me to prayer. Yet, it was a very self-interested prayer – God, sort out my problems! He responded and indicated a range of issues across my life that required my attention. But, still no conception. I had to conceive that God is no slot machine to service my felt needs.

As we enter nine days of prayer for God's will on earth, like Daniel we must fix our gaze on God and with uninterrupted intent pray not merely for our preferred needs, but for the grace of God throughout God's world.

Fasting and sackcloth sounds extreme, yet only if done to impress an audience. Daniel was intent on seeing the promises of God, revealed in the prophecy of Jeremiah, realised. It's strange the lengths we will go to secure something when we really want it. All the intrusive medical tests around fertility I went through, when I might just have trusted in God's provision.

As we start our prayer today, let's focus our attention on God. Let's set aside distractions and acknowledge the self-interest that too often motivates our prayer. Let's pause and simply pray for a world in need of God. Whenever I pray I always close with the words, 'Have mercy on us and the whole world; save us and the whole world'. Today let's together lift a fractured world to God for His blessing.

RELATED SCRIPTURE TO CONSIDER: Jer. 29:1–23; Psa. 33; Acts 17:22–32; Matt. 6:9–13.

AN ACTION TO TAKE: Ensure you always include a prayer for the world in which we live whenever you pray.

A PRAYER TO MAKE: 'Lord, You lived and died for everyone in our world. Today, hear my prayer for all who are vulnerable and be their strong defence. We pray with compassion for them every day. Amen.'

Daniel 9:1–6

'We have sinned and done wrong. We have been wicked and have rebelled; we have turned away from your commands and laws.' (v5)

Penitence is both sorrow for sins committed *and* a choice made to amend our way of life. It's repentance, a change of mind. My challenge is that I sincerely repent but then even as I rise from prayer my mind seizes hold of an impure thought or a criticism of someone else. How frustrating and tiresome! Yet what good news that God never tires of us returning to repent and extending complete forgiveness to us.

Daniel associates himself with the sins of the multitude, as we must. For only he who is without sin can cast aspersions! I am a sinner, so can make no judgment on others' behaviour. This would only be the odium of comparison. There is no hierarchy of sin; it is, and forever remains, simply sin.

Scripture reminds us that we've failed to listen and act upon information that would bring justice to many. We too often choose to live proclaiming Christ whilst serving self. Perhaps it's time to simply accept our common human condition, and make confession on behalf of sinful humanity and plead for God's forgiveness and deliverance in a world in serious trouble.

Like Daniel, let's reject reasoned analysis, a balance of good against bad, and boldly plead for God's forgiveness and deliverance. The world is in deep need of our prayer. Let's acknowledge our part in the source of its ills before we appeal to God for its salvation.

RELATED SCRIPTURE TO CONSIDER: 2 Chron. 7; 1 John 1:8–10; Prov. 28:12–14; Matt. 3:7–12.

AN ACTION TO TAKE: Start and end each day with a prayer of repentance. When troubled by temptation and sin, turn to God, pray and run from the source of the temptation.

A PRAYER TO MAKE: 'Lord, we're proud and arrogant, as individuals, families, churches and nations. Yet, You've still blessed us. Forgive us for taking Your blessing for granted. Amen.'

Shame

Daniel 9:7–8

'We and our kings, our princes and our ancestors are covered with shame, LORD, because we have sinned against you.' (v8)

Shame makes us feel uncomfortable. It speaks to all those actions and inner thoughts that we want to keep secret. It's about our sense of guilt and dishonour, feelings we recognise but too often choose to ignore. It causes confusion and often causes us to blush, an outward sign of inner discomfort.

As a teenager I volunteered for my local Oxfam. I campaigned for the starving in the world. Yet, I remain uncertain how much good was achieved. My question: to what extent was I serving my own need for self-approval? Was I acting self-righteously to compensate for my inner shame? I was, and remain, comfortable and cared for – whilst the hungry remain hungry to this day.

With God we're invited to become an open book. James criticises any form of faith that lacks substance. I rather like the tradition kept by some Christians of making my confession to someone else. This doesn't mean God cannot hear and forgive my private confession. Rather, it challenges me to 'come clean', to be transparent with a third party and name those thoughts and actions of which I am ashamed and embarrassed.

Shame, and our battle to bury its sources, dilutes our witness and hamstrings our service. We can't expect a fresh move of God whilst we stumble through life with dark secrets hidden, nor can acts of charity compensate for my shame. Our behaviour might look Christian, but in our heart are we truly submitted to God? Form without substance is living death.

RELATED SCRIPTURE TO CONSIDER: Psa. 32; James 1:19–27; 1 John 1:5–2:2; John 8:31–47.

AN ACTION TO TAKE: Shame seems insurmountable but is really a mirage. Read *Insight into Shame*: **edwj.org/mj21-16may**

A PRAYER TO MAKE: 'Lord, I renounce my shameful acts and thoughts and bring them into the light by confession to Jesus and trusted friends. I pray that You remove the shame of unfaithfulness from Your people. Amen.'

Daniel 9:9–12

'The Lord our God is merciful and forgiving, even though we have rebelled against him' (v9)

I t is a wonder my parents were capable of extending love towards me given my own love of disobedience and lying as a child. Only as I became a parent, adopted by a seven year old who was in our community, did I discover that a parent's love never releases the object of its love.

Great news! God loves us despite our deviant behaviours and sour attitudes aimed at Him and others. Our part is to respond to Him with complete surrender and frequent confession. Again I'm amazed at how quickly I return to sin following moments of deep connectedness with God. I'm reminded of the fracture of our fallen humanity.

If God can forgive me, then how can I refuse forgiveness to another, even one set upon my destruction? It's never easy in practice; yet remains God's way regardless of my feelings.

It is God's intention that our world is sustained in prayer 24/7. As our voices fade and we enter into sleep, others awaken to greet the dawn with their prayers. So we are to pray for everyone, regardless of our perspective, calling out to God for mercy and grace. Only as we dedicate ourselves to prayer, like those first disciples, can we expect the outpouring of God's Spirit, who alone transforms lives and complete situations. Prayer crafts the paths along which God's love and mercy flow throughout our world.

RELATED SCRIPTURE TO CONSIDER: Exod. 34:1–10; Psa. 25; Micah 7:14–20; Matt. 18:21–25.

AN ACTION TO TAKE: Make it your practice to pray a short prayer for God's grace for the whole world daily. Join with all those raising their voices around the clock for God's kingdom to come on earth.

A PRAYER TO MAKE: 'Lord, heal and bless our world. Bring comfort and hope as Your light pierces the darkness. Amidst the doom-and-gloom reality we pray that Your love will illuminate and forge a path for all. Amen.'

Become part of someone's testimony

Our Bible reading notes are read by hundreds of thousands of people around the world, and *Every Day with Jesus* and *Inspiring Women Every Day* have recently been made free in the UK. We want everyone, whatever their financial means, to have access to these resources that help them walk each day with our Saviour.

Here's what one *Every Day with Jesus* reader wrote to us:

Ever since I started using Everyday with Jesus, I reconnected to the Lord directly again. It deals with my day to day and minute to minute problems in details. Guiding me in the most solemn and right direction for a dedicated Christian living.

As we trust in God's provision, we know there are costs to providing this ministry. Do you have a passion for God's Word changing lives? Could supporting this vision be a way in which you serve?

A gift of just £2 a month from you will put daily Bible reading notes into the hands of at least one person who is hungry to know God and experience His presence every day.

Visit **waverleyabbeyresources.org/donate** to become part of someone's testimony, or use the form at the back of these notes.

Daniel 9:13–14

'Just as it is written in the Law of Moses, all this disaster has come on us, yet we have not sought the favour of the LORD our God by turning from our sins and giving attention to your truth.' (v13)

'Pay Attention!' A phrase that haunted me throughout my school days. How I hated the constraints of the classroom. The teacher would catch me gazing out of the window, daydreaming. I had little interest in listening and learning; I wanted to be outside. Interestingly, at university, one of my tutors boldly announced, 'Boots, not books, Jazz. Boots not books.' He had seen that my learning was through investigation rather than simply digesting the thoughts of others.

Obviously there's a balance. However, growing in God we are to pay attention to His instruction and then apply it to our life. School was an essential element in my growing up, yet knowledge that fails to inform behaviour yields a barren harvest.

We are to obey God in detail, for Scripture offers us the Maker's instructions for life. But these instructions are not simply for careful consideration or endless repetition. They are to enable Christ's disciples to follow in His footsteps and live the life of the kingdom as revealed in Scripture.

When implemented effectively, this offers a counter cultural expression to challenge the disasters experienced by so many. Will we choose to live in such a way as to offer the path to fullness of life to others? At the very least let's pray for them.

RELATED SCRIPTURE TO CONSIDER: Exod. 19:1–9; 2 Chron. 34; John 6:25–51; Col. 3:1–17.

AN ACTION TO TAKE: How can you take your Biblical understanding and turn it into everyday actions that reveal the life and love of Jesus, even when it means self-sacrifice?

A PRAYER TO MAKE: 'Lord, help me both to understand and to obey Your Word so that I reveal the character of the kingdom through my lifestyle and time-style. I pray that others would come to know You through my witness. Amen.'

Daniel 9:15–16

'Lord, in keeping with all your righteous acts, turn away your anger and your wrath from Jerusalem, your city, your holy hill. Our sins and the iniquities of our ancestors have made Jerusalem and your people an object of scorn to all those around us.' (v16)

We live in a world swamped with multiple 24/7 news feeds. That news is seldom good, or useful. What am I to do in the face of a severe earthquake or unprovoked attack on innocents? Information that I cannot process effectively and respond to with constructive action appears to me of little real value. I can empathise, but such empathy offers little comfort to the sufferer.

Scripture teaches that, 'The heart is deceitful above all things and beyond cure. Who can understand it?' (Jer. 17:9). My understanding of humanity's heart is as clearly revealed in Scripture. This state of the heart is perhaps why humanity is so often a source for bad news, and is most certainly an explanation for inhumanity.

We can make two key responses. The first is to work to ensure that our thoughts and actions reflect the character and nature of God. This we discover through reading God's Word and walking alongside His people. The second is to ensure that we set aside a regular time to pray to God on behalf of a world in great need.

Prayer is God's gift to us for turning the world the right way up. Living for Jesus means praying every day. Prayer is an irresistible, if invisible, force for good. We may feel – even see – little impact, yet Scripture assures us that prayer changes people's hearts, whilst holding back a vast tide of evil. A failure to pray will only compound the world's problems. Prayer is the Church's great gift to the welfare of humanity.

RELATED SCRIPTURE TO CONSIDER: Jer. 17:5–18; Psa. 14; Matt. 15:1–20; Eph. 6:10–20.

AN ACTION TO TAKE: Rather than clicking on a news channel, take those precious minutes to pray for God's mercy for a world in great need. Check a headline on your phone if you want a specific focus for your prayer, but then immediately pray.

A PRAYER TO MAKE: 'Lord, You know our world's woes. I pray for Your mercy and grace for all in need now. I also pray for Your people, however they are struggling today. Amen.'

Favour

Daniel 9:17–18

**'Now, our God, hear the prayers and petitions of your servant.
For your sake, Lord, look with favour on your
desolate sanctuary.' (v17)**

Reminding God to listen to our prayer requests is more a question of reassuring ourselves, because God has invited us to pray and promised to receive and respond. Yet, there's often a certain uncertainty within the human heart that God actually listens to our prayers.

One reason is the apparent lack of answers to our specific requests. In this there remains a great mystery, but it is through the heat of this mysterious storm that God is revealed. Caring for my first wife, Katey, I certainly called out for healing. I meant physical healing. This was not to be. However, as we persevered would either of us eventually have had it any other way? The short answer is no. For God's dealings with us were sweet in the very horrors of our experience and we gladly declared, 'It is well, it is well with my soul!'

I can no longer consult Katey since her death. But what God did in my life was truly amazing and I would be a fraction of the person I am today without the bitterness of that storm. God asks us to pray. Will we comply? Prayer is to secure God's purposes, many of which remain obscured to my human understanding. I pray, as I live, by faith not by sight.

Our prayers are always in accord with Jesus' own: 'not my will, but yours be done' (Luke 22:42).

RELATED SCRIPTURE TO CONSIDER: Jer. 33:1–3; Luke 22:39–46; 1 John 5:1–15; Psa. 139.

AN ACTION TO TAKE: It's hardest trusting God when personal requests are unanswered. But remember that you have surrendered your life to God, who is working His eternal purpose out through your life.

A PRAYER TO MAKE: 'Lord, "When peace like a river, attendeth my way, when sorrows like sea billows roll, whatever my lot, God teach me to say, it is well, it is well, with my soul." Amen.'

Listen, Forgive, Hear and Act

Daniel 9:19–21

'Lord, listen! Lord, forgive! Lord, hear and act! For your sake, my God, do not delay, because your city and your people bear your Name.' (v19)

I n lockdown I discovered the wonder of Zoom. Through Christmas, Waverley Abbey Resources held Evening Prayer sessions on Zoom. It was wonderful as people participated from all around the world.

I don't understand the technology, but gratefully use it. Equally, I don't understand prayer, but I gratefully pray daily for the benefits Scripture promises. It's remarkable that we can become involved in all God's doing in the world. We make a positive contribution through our prayers.

Prayer is simple and easy to engage with. God promises to listen, and simple requests such as 'Lord have mercy' impact the reality we inhabit. All distance between me and God is instantly removed as I confess my sin and receive God's forgiveness. Remember that King David, someone Scripture describes as a man after God's own heart, was a forgiven adulterer and murderer.

God hears our prayers, those of our lips and those of our heart. We are only ever expected to pray as we can, not as we can't. Prayer offers no graduate school, rather a space to stand face to face with our Lord. And, wonderfully, we can be assured that God hears and answers our prayers. However, that is something we choose to take on trust, for His ways are not our ways, as Isaiah reminds us.

RELATED SCRIPTURE TO CONSIDER: 1 Sam. 13:13–14; Isa. 55:6–13; Luke 18:9–14; Acts 13:14–43.

AN ACTION TO TAKE: Is there something specific you're concerned about in the world today? Agree to talk to God about this every day as your prayerful contribution to His purpose.

A PRAYER TO MAKE: 'Lord, I thank You for forgiving sin and listening to my prayers. Hear the prayers I make and take action that furthers Your will and purpose throughout our world. Amen.'

Daniel 9:22–27

'He instructed me and said to me, "Daniel, I have now come to give you insight and understanding."' (v22)

Scripture records events that can appear quite strange. They lie outside our normal, everyday experiences. Here, Daniel is greeted by the Angel Gabriel – the same angel who carried the news to Mary that she was to be the mother of Jesus.

Whilst I don't regularly hold conversations with angelic beings during my morning prayers, I do accept that whilst it may appear that I am simply standing, sitting or kneeling in my lounge, there is a far more important activity taking place. Unseen by the naked eye, I, together with all who pray, are participating in the constant conflict between God's purpose, that is guaranteed ultimate victory, and Satan's continuous, if fruitless, attempts to thwart it.

This is one reason I'm never surprised when my mind is distracted during prayer. I recognise that I've been daydreaming when intending to pray, or worrying about the day ahead, or even engaging in unholy thoughts!

The success of superhero movies convinces me that we all imagine a world of unseen forces influencing our life experience. Scripture teaches this isn't mere science fiction. We are ourselves engaged in a ferocious, often unseen, conflict. The influence of the evil we are up against can be observed in life's global terrors. As Christians, we are invited to collaborate in God's cause with our prayers and to secure ground in His eternal purpose.

RELATED SCRIPTURE TO CONSIDER: 2 Cor. 10:2–6; 1 Tim. 2:1–8; 2 Tim. 2:1–13; 1 Pet. 5:8–9.

AN ACTION TO TAKE: Many fellow Christians are today persecuted for their faith. Take time to learn about, and pray for, the challenges others face around the world. Visit **edwj.org/mj21-22may**

A PRAYER TO MAKE: 'Lord, I pray for all those throughout the world who are suffering on account of their faith. Strengthen, sustain and set free Your suffering church. Amen.'

Acts 2:1–4

'All of them were filled with the Holy Spirit and began to speak in other tongues as the Spirit enabled them.' (v4)

Pentecost celebrates the birth of the Church. The angel told the disciples to gather in Jerusalem and there to wait and pray. After nine days the Holy Spirit hovered over them and they were all filled with the Holy Spirit.

The Christian life is a challenge without the action of the Holy Spirit. I know for a number of years as a new Christian, I struggled. I faithfully prayed and read my Bible. I attended a beginner's group for fellowship and teaching. However, I was struggling to maintain, even make sense of, my faith. It seemed very dry and I appeared to be fulfilling my duty with little enthusiasm.

Then I encountered the person of the Holy Spirit. Like those first disciples the Spirit had been present within me, yet not released in power. Jesus, full of the Spirit after baptism, was led into the wilderness by the same Spirit, yet returned, after His trials, in the power of the Spirit.

Life is demanding. The unseen battle to advance the kingdom of God is a continual struggle. But we have not been abandoned. The Holy Spirit fills and accompanies us every day, always pointing us, and others, to Jesus, whilst revealing God in us. My choice is always choosing between accommodating this world's values and causes or praying and serving the interests of God for the extent of my life on earth.

RELATED SCRIPTURE TO CONSIDER: Acts 1:6–11; Luke 4:1–14; John 20:19–23; Luke 12:1–12.

AN ACTION TO TAKE: Today is Pentecost. You have walked the nine days of prayer. Decide today if you want to yield to God afresh, or for the first time. Ask to be filled with the power of the Holy Spirit of Truth, Hope and Love.

A PRAYER TO MAKE: 'Spirit of the Living God, fall afresh on me; melt me, mould me, fill me, use me. Spirit of the living God, fall afresh on me.' (Daniel Iverson The UM Hymnal, No. 393.)

Write to **micha@edwj.org** and I'll write back personally and in confidence as soon as I can.

Acts 2:5–13

Amazed and perplexed, they asked one another, "What does this mean?"' (v12)

I n both Old and New Testaments an encounter with God led to change. Here, the frightened, despondent disciples found a confidence and courage in God to describe the source of their faith. Over the years, the Church seems slowly to have lost its confidence and courage. It tends to answer questions no-one's asking. Very different from that first Pentecost!

Last year, facing the start of a global pandemic, navigating lockdown with its threat to our mental wellbeing, economic viability and family life, the Christian voice appeared silenced. I'm not talking of the move from in-person to virtual services or the continuance of ministries such as food banks, often, but not solely, operated by local congregations. No, I was shocked at what I perceived to be a lack of national Christian leadership.

In a time when social media offers a platform for every perspective – many with unhealthy political objectives or just ugly irresponsibility – we, Jesus' friends, appeared to absent ourselves from the public discourse. At Waverley Abbey Resources, in response to God's call to continue the ministry as a voice to encourage living every day with Jesus, we want to join with others to restore that national and even international Christian voice. A ministry encouraging everyone that God is alive and in touch with people. To proclaim that, accept Him or reject Him, God's Spirit can move mountains in response to the prayers of God's people.

RELATED SCRIPTURE TO CONSIDER: Hab. 3; 1 Kings 19:1–18; Acts 19:1–10; Eph. 5:14–20.

AN ACTION TO TAKE: Be encouraged by the first Christians in Acts with the power of Jesus' message. Be encouraged in your faith and empowered by the Holy Spirit. Visit **edwj.org/mj21-24may**

A PRAYER TO MAKE: 'Lord, I invite You to fill me daily with Your Spirit that I might be a change agent where I live and amongst my family, friends and work colleagues. Amen.'

Acts 2:14–21

'Then Peter stood up with the Eleven, raised his voice and addressed the crowd: "Fellow Jews and all of you who live in Jerusalem, let me explain this to you; listen carefully to what I say."' (v14)

I've worked twenty years as a professional mediator. Whilst my call is to prayer and nurturing faith, this provided my income for a long time. Mediation (working with people to resolve real conflict) requires a lot of active listening. In this context the word 'listen' means to hear, heed and obey; three actions.

So Peter says, 'listen carefully'. Often when mediating, the conflicted parties can only hear what they expect to hear. They're incapable of heeding the intention and purpose behind what's being said. They are glued to their perspective, seeing the other person as *the* problem. Now, it's important to realise that we can never forcibly change another person. We can only ever change ourselves.

Peter hears from the Spirit, heeds His word and obeys. He addresses the crowd and says, 'Listen, we're not drunk and Jesus is more than an executed felon. He is in fact risen, alive and offering an eternal relationship.'

Filled with the Spirit, these first disciples heard, heeded and obeyed. They became God's voice to overturn false perceptions of Himself and create opportunities for faith by making peace with Him, our Creator. The Spirit still empowers Jesus' disciples, you and me, for the same purpose. Are we willing to stand up alongside those first disciples? We have the opportunity to challenge false perceptions about God by hearing, heeding and obeying.

RELATED SCRIPTURE TO CONSIDER: Deut. 13:1–5; Prov. 16:17–25; Matt. 7:24–27; James 1:19–25.

AN ACTION TO TAKE: Learning to listen – hear, heed and obey – takes time. Commit to listening to God's voice in Scripture, in the Church (past and present) and in prayer. Live the God-life.

A PRAYER TO MAKE: 'Lord, I want to listen. Speak clearly as I'm surrounded by so many calls on my time and energy. I choose to follow and live for You alone. Amen.'

Acts 2:22–23

'Fellow Israelites, listen to this: Jesus of Nazareth was a man accredited by God to you by miracles, wonders and signs, which God did among you through him, as you yourselves know.' (v22)

My reluctance to speak up for Jesus comes from my embarrassment. In a world where rationality rules, it's hard to speak, and to be taken seriously, when describing that which lies beyond reason.

Whilst there is a clear rational basis for the gospel, faith and God's Kingdom currency always remains beyond rationality. For, as Scripture declares, faith is the unseen hope for and by which we choose to live.

Can we embrace a miracle-working Messiah, risen from the dead and capable of building a personal relationship today? This was Peter's proclamation; one that laid the foundation for the first church. It remains the core of our Christian belief. It alone offers hope to a despondent world.

Our Christian confession only reflects the confidence we have in God. This is always tested through life's challenges. Yet, we alone can make the choice to maintain such confidence in a supernatural God – whilst only a supernatural God can offer a source of fresh hope and inspiration to our world.

Time hasn't diminished God's power. Jesus remains the same yesterday, today and forever; He's still accredited by God by miracles. I have a testimony of the miracle of new life, a testimony I can freely share if I dare. Do I so dare? And do you have such a testimony, and will you dare alongside me?

RELATED SCRIPTURE TO CONSIDER: Heb. 13:7–10; Eph. 3:14–21; Prov. 3:1–12; Psa. 20:6–9.

AN ACTION TO TAKE: It takes courage to stand one's ground as a Christian. But if you lose confidence in God you cannot take faith filled decisions based on God's Word. Consider this: will you stand for Jesus, however inconvenient it seems?

A PRAYER TO MAKE: 'Lord, I choose to stand upon the truth of Your Word. Help me to withstand the criticism of a world built upon rationality alone. Amen.'

Bouncing Forwards

By Patrick Regan

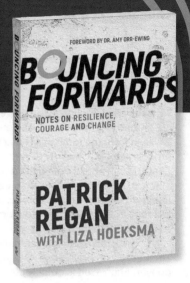

'You'll bounce back.'

Have you ever heard those words? They are always well-meant, but there's one problem: why would we want to bounce back? When what we go through teaches us so much, why would we want to return to how we were before? Perhaps there's a better option. Let's bounce forwards instead.

Explore what true resilience is, and reflect on themes of courage, change and emotional agility as Patrick shares from his own experience and the experiences of others. Readers will also benefit from an included bonus devotional, 'The Resilient Life' by Diane Regan.

'Masterfully woven together' – Tanya Marlow

'A brilliant, timely book for everyone' – Pete Greig

'This book is utterly life-giving' – Will Van Der Hart

'Disarmingly honest and powerfully vulnerable'
– Malcolm Duncan

Start your journey in bouncing forwards today at
waverleyabbeyresources.org/bf

Patrick Regan OBE is Co-Founder of Kintsugi Hope. He is author of six books and speaks regularly on TV and radio on issues of faith, justice and wellbeing.

Acts 2:24–36

'But God raised him from the dead, freeing him from the agony of death, because it was impossible for death to keep its hold on him.' (v23)

Jesus' resurrection is the hinge of history. Killed on an executioner's gibbet, this man, who was equally God, broke the curse of death and rose from the tomb. It's remarkable that I feel embarrassed by what others might make of my Christian faith when humanity's greatest fear, death, lies in abject defeat at the foot of the cross.

Again, it's a remarkable story because we do not expect people to rise from death. Jesus of course, unlike Lazarus, wasn't restored to life, but rose in a new, resurrected form; hence His command to Mary, 'Do not touch me!' (John. 20:17).

I recently ran a series of seminars with a friend entitled, 'Death: The Last Great Adventure'. Death, it seems, is not subject to popular conversation. God is quickly dismissed, but irrational reactions to death remain. If we are merely mortals, composed of nothing more than six elements, oxygen, carbon, hydrogen, nitrogen, calcium and phosphorus, why are we intimidated by death? Surely it would be merely part of life's natural process and to be seen rationally and non-emotionally.

However, God declares that death offers a portal to a life lived with the Creator of the universe forever. And herein lies the choice facing each one of us, and the heart of our Christian message of hope: will we choose eternity with or separated from God? As Paul declared, to live is Christ, to die is gain (Phil. 1:21).

RELATED SCRIPTURE TO CONSIDER: Isa. 26:16–21; John 11:1–43; John 20:11–18; Phil. 1:12–26.

AN ACTION TO TAKE: Reflect upon your own mortality and your fears of death. Maybe, like me, you have lost someone very dear. How have you processed this with God and others?

A PRAYER TO MAKE: 'Lord, my eternity is safe with You. I pray that my family, friends and neighbours might find assurance in You for themselves. Amen.'

Repent and be Baptised

Acts 2:37–38

'Peter replied, "Repent and be baptised, every one of you, in the name of Jesus Christ for the forgiveness of your sins. And you will receive the gift of the Holy Spirit."' (v38)

Response is always a matter of our will. We are masters of our personal choices. Poor choices can create habits and fears that cause dither and delay. Yet, I'm created for choices, which determine my life's course.

I can easily make bad choices, which have unexpected consequences. These I hadn't bargained on, but I must live with the repercussions. Good choices also have unanticipated consequences. Our choices affect out reality. It's in dealing with all the consequences that character is forged.

I've married twice. Katey, my first wife, sadly died of progressive MS after eighteen years. Jayne, my current wife, has a complex of chronic health conditions, which have a major impact on our life together. Lessons learnt with Katey have forged some character that helps. Whilst Jayne faces her own daily faith decisions as she handles the impact of her health. What shall we learn individually and together?

Character is always forged from our decisions. My understanding of the Christian path is today so different from when I first encountered Jesus. But the intimacy and deep confidence I enjoy in that friendship with God today is the fruit of the expected as well as the unanticipated consequences of my life choices.

I know the choices I have already made but what of those I have still to take?

RELATED SCRIPTURE TO CONSIDER: John 1:29–50; Luke 9:18–27; Isa. 40:21–41; Psa. 126.

AN ACTION TO TAKE: In deciding to repent and be baptised, you make a choice to follow God's way. It's no guarantee against misadventure, but it does assure You of finding a way through by God's grace and encouragement.

A PRAYER TO MAKE: 'Lord, there are times when I despair in my circumstances. Yet, I've chosen Your way. Lead me on and build my character each step of the way. Amen.'

Acts 2:39–41

The promise is for you and your children and for all who are far off – for all whom the Lord our God will call.' (v39)

I n the past, I've made the mistake of assuming the Christian life about my personal development. Sadly, Christianity is no self-improvement programme. Remarkably, in an increasingly self-absorbed society, Christian discipleship can easily become an end in itself, rather than the path along which I travel ever deeper into God's embrace

Archbishop Temple stated that the Church was the only society existing entirely for the benefit of its non-members. It's why Jesus tells us to love our neighbours to the degree that we love ourselves and Paul encourages us to put the interests of others above our own. That is counter cultural today.

Personal tragedy hijacked my life but that demanded I face up to who I was, and, most importantly, who Jesus really is. I am grateful that a period of personal pain gave birth to a life of prayer and devotion to God. I hate to think how pompous and self-referential I'd have been today without this God interrupting me in this way.

The joy of Jesus' message of love and hope is that no-one is excluded. However, no-one knows this reality until and unless we, the Christian community, share it with them through our lives as much as our words. Words come all too easily to me; life choices involving generosity, kindness and care require effort. I'm not always in that frame of mind. I want to take care of myself, yet God reminds us that all our needs have been catered for through redemption. Dare we live like this?

RELATED SCRIPTURE TO CONSIDER: Lev. 19:9–19; Luke 10:25–37; Lev. 19:33–34; James 1:22–27.

AN ACTION TO TAKE: 'The first question the priest and the Levite asked was: "If I stop to help this man, what will happen to me?" But the good Samaritan reversed the question: "If I do not stop to help, what will happen to this man?"' Think about your response to this Martin Luther King quote.

A PRAYER TO MAKE: 'Lord, help me to love my neighbour as I love myself, and put their interests ahead of my own. Amen.'

Acts 2:42–47

'They devoted themselves to the apostles' teaching and to fellowship, to the breaking of bread and to prayer.' (v42)

Last Christmas was challenging. Jayne and I spent it alone for the first time. Covid-19 regulations prevented us gathering as a family. Yet, we discovered great joy where we'd first anticipated sadness. Much like that stable, hardly an appropriate birthing suite, joy replaced apparent deprivation, and we found Christ and hope afresh in our anticipated sorrow.

Scripture reveals the work of the Christian family: prayer, teaching and friendship through communion with God and each other. Family is so fragmented today. Many yearn for family whilst it is truly found in our fellowship together in Christ.

Friendship with God is never solo love; it's belonging to an enlightened community, expressing healthy relationships and extending welcome to those bruised and beaten by life experience. If we took time to once again craft such communities of welcome, hospitality, hope and healing, we might expect to find favour with a lost and lonely world. Many would earnestly seek the God who facilitates family.

This is the objective reality that best indicates revival is arriving, and we will continue our journey looking at how we might best lay the foundations upon which God's Spirit might raise up a fresh revival within our own day.

RELATED SCRIPTURE TO CONSIDER: Eccl. 4:1–12; Psa. 146; 1 Pet. 2:9–17; Rom. 12:9–21.

AN ACTION TO TAKE: Re-read today's verse and consider how you can live and express it more effectively in fellowship with others.

A PRAYER TO MAKE: 'Lord, I pray that I may work with Your Holy Spirit in laying foundations for a fresh outpouring of Your love. Amen.'

Wait for God

Exodus 32:1–9

'When the people saw that Moses was so long in coming down from the mountain, they gathered round Aaron and said, "Come, make us gods who will go before us. As for this fellow Moses who brought us up out of Egypt, we don't know what has happened to him."' (v1)

It's essential that we wait for God's revelation alone. As the disciples awaited the Holy Spirit, they chose an apostle, Mattias, by lot. Was this human action or divine inspiration? Mattias was appointed before the disciples were baptised in the Spirit, and not by Jesus. This is his one appearance in Scripture.

There's a danger when left to our own devices that we fill times of waiting for God with ideas born of human ingenuity. This is always our choice and challenge: to trust God or rely upon ourselves.

The Israelites, waiting for Moses to return from his sojourn with God on Mount Horeb, decided to take matters into their own hands. Aaron, perhaps intimidated by the crowd of restless Israelites, fails to withstand their demands, preferring to placate human impatience rather than plead for God's presence.

Church history is littered with plans born of human ingenuity, requiring energy and resources, which advanced God's kingdom not one centimetre. This remains true today, when the crafting of schemes to further God's cause knows no limit. Impatience is a human weakness; God asks that we wait, watch and pray. In His good time there will be the visitation of God's Spirit, who alone can usher in authentic expressions of God's kingdom on earth.

RELATED SCRIPTURE TO CONSIDER: Acts 1:12–26; 1 Sam. 13:1–15; Heb. 10:19–39; Psa. 130.

AN ACTION TO TAKE: Impatience is to be restless with current circumstances. God's promise is trustworthy and He invites us to wait in patient trust. Is this invitation one you need to accept?

A PRAYER TO MAKE: 'Lord, in repentance and rest is my salvation and in quietness and trust is my strength. Help me to cultivate patience throughout my life.' (See Isaiah 30:15.)

Exodus 3:1–12

'There the angel of the LORD appeared to him in flames of fire from within a bush. Moses saw that though the bush was on fire it did not burn up.' (v2)

How can we recognise God's presence? Here Moses does what he'd done hundreds of times: he take his flocks to pasture. A shepherd is responsible for feeding his flock and keeping them safe from injury and assault. He's in the shadow of Mount Horeb, where he would one day again encounter God for the Ten Commandments.

What's true for Moses is true for us. As we engage with the everyday, God will speak to us. Perhaps not through an inexplicable, non-consumed burning bush, but always with the unexpected interruption that symbolises the Spirit's presence.

It's one reason for patience in all things, because if we hurry through those chores we dislike we may pass by God's interruption unnoticed. Hence, I've learnt to look for God in all my daily experiences, from creating breakfast, to doing the laundry, to cleaning and stacking the dishes. In such moments we often encounter that still, small voice of God.

The only purpose worth living for is the one God has for your life – and this isn't determined by society's preference for wealth or celebrity status. This is about uncovering the call implanted by God from the moment of our creation. Happiness is never in accumulation; it's in letting go of self and grasping God. This is what an anxious Moses encountered unexpectedly as he went about his business.

RELATED SCRIPTURE TO CONSIDER: 1 Kings 19:1–18; Hab. 3:1–2 & 16–19; Luke 10:25–37; Luke 12:35–48.

AN ACTION TO TAKE: Reflect on your life with God so far. At what points have you encountered Him and taken decisions that have impacted the choices you have made?

A PRAYER TO MAKE: 'Lord, let me meet You in the everyday realities of my life and then choose what is right and of You. Amen.'

Exodus 3:13 – 4:17

'God said to Moses, "I AM WHO I AM. This is what you are to say to the Israelites: 'I AM has sent me to you.'"' (3:14)

It's easier to criticise than to encourage. Our daughter thrives on encouragement. At parents' evenings I easily worked out in which subjects she'd flourish: those taught by teachers who motivated by encouragement, not criticism. Media quickly creates a negative narrative, from fears over Brexit to a global pandemic. In contrast, the gospel is GOOD NEWS! It's good news for us and for all. So we need to live as good-news people.

Moses, no doubt uncertain of his safety in Egypt, and filled with human insecurity, pushes God's patience to its limit, save for the fact that it's limitless! In response, God encourages Moses with each hesitation. Ultimately, God is left with no option but to challenge Moses' commitment.

Our challenge? It's this: how committed am I to living the good news? It's easy to be a beneficiary, yet the benefits are equally for others. As disciples we present a window through which others can gaze upon the kingdom of God.

Francis Schaeffer characterised our society as the selfish pursuit of personal peace and affluence. Jesus daily disturbs us with a challenge to pray and work in the interests of an altogether different kingdom. One into which we're enrolled as citizens by virtue of our faith. Moses I'm sure might have preferred to remain in Jethro's service, but God had other plans. Only Moses might decide who he would serve with his life.

RELATED SCRIPTURE TO CONSIDER: Isa. 41:8–20; Lam. 3:19–27; John 4:1–26; John 8:1–11.

AN ACTION TO TAKE: God believes in you and invites you to live the kingdom life. Do you believe in yourself? Consider God's Word, full of encouragement spoken personally to you.

A PRAYER TO MAKE: 'Lord, let us not lose heart. Let us fix our eyes not on what is seen, but on what is unseen, since what is seen is temporary, but what is unseen is eternal. Amen.' (2 Cor. 4:18.)

Simply Church

– New Edition

By Sim Dendy

With new chapter on the Church in crisis, 'Weathering the Storm', written during Covid-19.

When crisis strikes – such as the Covid-19 pandemic – we have no choice but to stop and assess where we are. Our world needs the Church, like never before, to be full of hope. But the Church is not always what it could be. Perhaps we need a declutter. A clear-out. A detox.

This book is for all people who are passionate about the Church of Jesus Christ and seeing it continue to grow and serve.

We all collect excess stuff – books, clothes, cars, gadgets… thoughts, habits, scars, traditions… Sometimes, it's good to strip things back a bit. It's healthy to occasionally explore our past and consider a fresh purpose for the future.

To realign ourselves with the plan that our creator God has already set out for us.

To recalibrate.

To return to the start again.

To go back a couple of millennia to discover what the original Church looked like, so we can remember and reset.

Simply… Church.

To find out more and to purchase, visit **waverleyabbeyresources.org/sc**

Exodus 4:18–31

'Then Moses went back to Jethro his father-in-law and said to him, "Let me return to my own people in Egypt to see if any of them are still alive." Jethro said, "Go, and I wish you well."' (v18)

Converted at university, God called me into evangelism. So I volunteered with Youth for Christ – full-time ministry was voluntary in my day! My father, proud I'd gone to Oxford, had negotiated a place for me in a city accountancy firm. I turned it down. This created a very difficult relationship between my dad and me for five years and we hardly spoke.

Saying yes to God may well mean saying no to someone or something else. Serving God comes with no five-star promises. I remember meeting some Syrian Christians who spoke with pride at the honour given to their family members when beheaded by ISIS. My shocked expression caused them to comfort me with encouraging words that this is the fruit that serving God may yield.

If we seek revival, a fresh outpouring of God's love, presence and power, then it comes with a price tag attached. It demands complete obedience to all God says, and with no guarantees except knowing we are serving God. That's a big ask.

Moses gave up the life he'd known to explore the uncharted path of obedience. Decisions can only be made in the present – we can only live in the present tense. The future is God's responsibility. If I'm tempted to look to my future, I can only do so by taking my eyes off God. Christian service is a full-time occupation for everyone, here and now.

RELATED SCRIPTURE TO CONSIDER: Prov. 16:1–9; 1 Kings 8:54–61; Phil. 3:7–21; Matt. 6:25–34.

AN ACTION TO TAKE: Service will demand sacrifice. Yet, we simply walk in the footsteps of Jesus who surrendered all in order to win all.

A PRAYER TO MAKE: 'Lord, may I daily live a life of sacrificial service by faith in Jesus, who loves me and gave Himself for me. Amen.'

Plead with God

Exodus 32:7–14

'But Moses sought the favour of the LORD his God. "LORD," he said, "why should your anger burn against your people, whom you brought out of Egypt with great power and a mighty hand?" (v11)

A t the heart of every strong, healthy relationship lies effective communication. The most important relationship any one of us has is with God and this relies upon regular communication, or prayer.

Here, God is angry and threatens to destroy a disobedient people. Moses rejects taking a self-righteous stance.

How often have I celebrated another's discomfort, even failure? Why is it that my humanity instinctively enjoys the gossip about someone else's failure? Scripture reminds me I am fractured and completely dependent upon God; the good that I do is no more than filthy rags.

Like Moses, if we are to see God intervene afresh in this world, two things are required. First we must humble ourselves, setting aside the self-made masks that disguise the darker aspects of our nature and intentions. God knows all, so consistently sees behind our masks.

Second, we are to pray on behalf of others, without judgment, pleading for God to bring salvation, restore hope and maintain peace and order throughout our troubled world. Prayer offers the invisible supports that sustain God's mercy, which benefits us all. God alone has the capacity to quell chaos. We have the privileged responsibility of pleading with God for a continuance of such mercy and order against a backdrop of sin and selfishness.

RELATED SCRIPTURE TO CONSIDER: Isa. 1:11–23; Deut. 9:15–19; 1 Tim. 2:1–8; Eph. 6:10–18.

AN ACTION TO TAKE: Prayer is a hidden force that secures the purpose of God on earth. When do you pray? What resources do you need?

A PRAYER TO MAKE: 'Lord, I pray and plead that in every situation the peace of God might guard all hearts and minds in Christ Jesus. Amen.'

Exodus 33:12–23

'Then Moses said to him, "If your Presence does not go with us, do not send us up from here."' (v15)

How wonderful it is that the creator of the universe is ready to instruct us in how to live. I could not have wished for a richer life experience than God has kindly given to me. Yet, none of us find it easy.

Caring for my wife for eighteen years as she was destroyed by progressive MS forced me to measure my natural human response to God's invited response. I was all self-pity; God, all compassion. I was swift to anger; God, our calm in the storm. I grew despondent; God offered hope. We needed God's presence and to learn to practice the presence of God at all times.

The challenge is always learning to live like Jesus, never just increased knowledge of God. 'Christian' means 'little Christ'. Initially a term of derision, it came to symbolise those who prayed and cared for everyone, regardless of who they were.

Church history tells us a lot. Pandemics aren't new. From the earliest days the world was silenced as Christians chose to love neighbours practically, remaining with those with the plague, even though it meant sacrificing their own lives. Government guidelines may change, but Jesus' command to love and serve our neighbour must always be considered.

How like Jesus these people were: incarnate, fleshing out the message of love and hope, whatever the cost. Our challenge is in God's invitation to live like Jesus. Through prayer and God's Word, we can become who God created us to be, for it is no longer I who live, but Christ who lives in me!

RELATED SCRIPTURE TO CONSIDER: Ezek. 34:1–10; Acts 11:19–30; Mat. 25:31–46; Gal. 6:1–9.

AN ACTION TO TAKE: What does living every day with Jesus require from you?

A PRAYER TO MAKE: 'Lord, help us to live as an expression of sacrificial love at home, at work and in our communities. Amen.'

Exodus 34:27–32

'Afterwards all the Israelites came near him, and he gave them all the commands the LORD had given him on Mount Sinai.' (v32)

We read God's Word to grow in our understanding of both who God is and who we are in His sight and purpose. We must never forget that we are in this world to serve that purpose. Paul tells Timothy that his first responsibility is to live by the rules God has given. These are clearly set out in Scripture.

These rules are presented in two forms. There is a list of 'dos and don'ts', such as the Ten Commandments. Although given to Moses, they still apply to us today as we serve God. Then there's the more challenging issue of defeating those temptations (or, as the Early Church named them, 'our appetites') that seek to divert us from God's business and focus on our own interests.

Without mastering our natural appetites, we shall never live comfortably by God's rules. Indeed there's vast literature stretching across the centuries describing the Christian disciple's struggle with what Scripture calls 'the flesh', from the Latin *caro*, meaning carnal. It's the squeeze each of us encounters. The decisions we take demonstrate the degree to which we live for God in practice. This in turn influences the likelihood of any fresh outpouring of God's grace.

Of course, if we are again to see God move in revival, we must acknowledge the many flaws that undermine our confidence in Him and eat away at a robust Christian faith. Our next task is to consider how God invites us to do this.

RELATED SCRIPTURE TO CONSIDER: Gen. 4:6–12; Deut. 28:1–24; 2 Tim. 1–7; Heb. 12:1–13.

AN ACTION TO TAKE: All of us feel defensive and ashamed of those temptations that rule our thoughts and behaviour. Yet, God knows them all and we must choose if we will exercise the discipline to overcome them. We may need some professional support.

A PRAYER TO MAKE: 'Lord, I pray that, by Your grace, I may actively engage in defeating those things that draw me away from You. Amen.'

Exodus 40:16–33
'Moses did everything just as the LORD commanded him.' (v16)

Eight times it's written that Moses did as the Lord commanded. God is interested in detail, not just the big picture. We easily ignore 'incidental' steps, and assume we're obeying God.

In Revelation, God challenged six of seven churches with the fatal flaw that quenched the Spirit, raising questions about their faithfulness. As disciples we are filled with God's Spirit. We are vehicles through whom God exposes and contests evil in society. Our lives offer a critical window through which people can gaze upon the kingdom of God. In light of this, do we have flaws to address?

The risen Jesus stands and intercedes beside His Father for the gospel to be made visible through the lives of His people. The angel declares to each of the seven churches in Revelation, 'Whoever has ears, let them hear what the Spirit says to the churches' (Rev. 3:22), a phrase found on Jesus' lips also (Matt. 11:15).

We don't require an angel to mobilise our faith. We have the witness and ministry of Jesus; we have God's carefully spoken Word; we enjoy access to God's throne of grace. It's about how we choose to live, and it's the minutiae of our lives that God is interested in. It's what's perhaps invisible to family and friends and too easily brushed aside by us, yet studied by God. It's often said that the devil is in the detail, and that is something to seriously consider in our Christian lives.

RELATED SCRIPTURE TO CONSIDER: Rev. 2–3; Josh. 7:1–12; Mark 4:9; Heb. 4:8–16.

AN ACTION TO TAKE: Carry out a swift audit of your life, especially what might count as the minutiae, and ask yourself: am I living in every way as the Lord commands me to?

A PRAYER TO MAKE: 'Lord, you know my deeds, my hard work and my perseverance. Reveal anything where I am resisting You, so that I may be a window into Your kingdom through my life. Amen.'

Luke 18:9–14

'But the tax collector stood at a distance. He would not even look up to heaven, but beat his breast and said, "God, have mercy on me, a sinner."' (v13)

Our age celebrates self-confidence and self-help: 'I' am the source of my inner angst and many teach that the choices 'I' make determine 'my' success or failure. While there may lie a kernel of truth here, God's kingdom turns such popular wisdom upside down.

Each of us must learn to make our way in life. But while some seem to be naturally at an advantage in many areas; others, through lack of opportunity, or sickness or disability, have an apparent unfair disadvantage. This again reveals God's immense grace. For in God's sight we are all equal. He sees the condition of our spiritual state and is entirely disinterested in what society deems our advantage or disadvantage.

The fullness of life Jesus describes is making peace with God and serving others. Here we realise our purpose. The challenge lies in finding the humility to accept ourselves for who and how we are, whilst receiving God's love and affirmation.

My pride was crushed when moving from a platform evangelist to a domestic carer. I initially focused upon my disappointment and frustration. I cared only for myself! Yet God reminded me that I was dependent upon His care, secured at great price. I came to see my new role as a gift, and indeed my core purpose. I recognised how much my pride and self-interest had driven me. I had to decide to move from standing with the Pharisee to taking my place alongside the tax collector. The process hurt, but it healed.

RELATED SCRIPTURE TO CONSIDER: Prov. 22:1–11; Micah 6:6–8; John 10:1–10; Rom. 2:1–11.

AN ACTION TO TAKE: Humility is constantly assaulted by an inner desire to justify ourselves. The tax collector kept it simple. He was disliked within society, yet loved by God, and comfortable with an honest assessment of his need.

A PRAYER TO MAKE: 'Lord, help me to live with no need to justify myself but simply to declare, "God, have mercy on me, a sinner". Amen.'

John 4:1–42

'Many of the Samaritans from that town believed in him because of the woman's testimony, "He told me everything I've ever done."' (v39)

D. M. Panton describes revival as 'the inrush of divine life into a body threatening to become a corpse' (*Revival* by D. M. Panton). Revival is a wake-up call to the promised purpose and presence of God on earth. It is the Church returning to Pentecost. Certainly the Samaritan woman woke up to the person and life of Jesus. Such was her testimony that her disapproving neighbours wanted what she'd discovered.

I'm personally tired of apologising for Christ and our Christian faith. A secular media, together with a social environment that consistently undermines authority, devalues committed relationships and worships the pursuit of self-interest, has rejected God's order and seeks to undermine God's Word.

Yet, this story demonstrates how God's truth breaks into broken circumstances to bring hope, joy and healing. Only with God can hope be both realised and sustained. It's not our context that shapes us, but who shares that context with us. Revival consists of a deep awareness of our need for God, together with a sense of our shortcomings. This is accompanied by a deep desire for a fresh start, no matter who we are or what we've done.

God is no respecter of social convention or status. He invites us, like Jesus, to draw alongside our community and introduce its members to the living water that quenches our persistent thirst for Truth.

RELATED SCRIPTURE TO CONSIDER: Psalm 85; Isa. 57:11–21; Acts 2:36–41; 1 John 1:5–10.

AN ACTION TO TAKE: Consider this: does our faith stand in need of a spring clean? If we cannot perceive the outpouring of God's love throughout society, maybe our spiritual lens needs a Holy Spirit polish!

A PRAYER TO MAKE: 'Lord, I pray for Holy Spirit power, that I may live as your witness wherever life carries me. Amen.'

Mark 2:13–17

'When the teachers of the law who were Pharisees saw him eating with the sinners and tax collectors, they asked his disciples: "Why does he eat with tax collectors and sinners?"' (v16)

Jesus walked the Holy Land with a simple call, 'Come! Follow me'. A variety of individuals responded. I wonder how many declined His invitation?

The call was for anyone, and it still is today. If ever there was an equitable society, it is God's kingdom because the only membership criterion is acknowledging one's sinfulness, which infects us all. No wonder some were shocked at who they saw Jesus associating with.

Matthew was a tax collector. For the Jews under Roman rule he was a 'quisling', a traitor collaborating with an occupying army. He was also an offence to the religious leaders of the day. So how could a moral religious teacher associate with sinners? But that's the point! God has made sinners His special interest. That's the good news.

For each disciple, following Jesus demanded a complete change of direction. Perhaps many of us today are not called away from our chosen profession, although we are told to hold lightly to it and its benefits. We accept an invitation to go where God leads and live serving His interests first and foremost. Like those first disciples our natural assumptions and preferences are disturbed as we struggle with how to live by faith alone. Revival, always a result of fervent, lived faith, awaits a people who've deliberately chosen whole-heartedly to follow Jesus in every aspect of their lives.

RELATED SCRIPTURE TO CONSIDER: Deut. 24:10–19; Zech. 7; Luke 14:15–24; Gal. 5:1–13.

AN ACTION TO TAKE: At what points in your life have you chosen to shut your ears to God's call? No matter; respond with all that you feel able to entrust of your life to God today in response to His call.

A PRAYER TO MAKE: 'Lord, help me when You call me to change direction in response to Your call. Amen.'

FRIDAY 11 JUNE

Shaken and Stirred

Acts 4:23–31

'After they prayed, the place where they were meeting was shaken. And they were all filled with the Holy Spirit and spoke the word of God boldly.' (v31)

I've not attended a prayer meeting shaken by God, but as a friend says, 'Never say never!' If we live by faith, today is what counts; where is God present? Peter and John had seen a man healed who had been unable to walk, and faced detention for a breach of the peace and been released – their crime unique and outside legal precedent.

The authorities were also amazed at the courage and coherent message of two 'unschooled' and unremarkable men (v13). In fact the unremarkable made space for our remarkable God. Pentecost in action! The disciples found their confidence in God's provision, and we're invited to do the same.

Without God's inspiration, the man who could not walk would have been left to beg, and the authorities free to crush the Church. When facing the impossible, Peter and John called upon the name of Jesus (Acts 3:6) and God intervened to create a grace moment.

Believing Peter and John would have self-preservation uppermost in their minds, and hoping they'd be frightened by their arrest, the authorities released them on condition they'd not speak in Jesus' name again. Peter and John were faced with a choice we have to make: were they – and are we – to obey the voice of self-interest or the voice of God?

Uncertain of what tomorrow might bring, they gathered with the believers and prayed both for protection, but also for more of God. That's the fertiliser for all revival: praying for more of God.

RELATED SCRIPTURE TO CONSIDER: Esther 4:6–17; Psa. 13; Luke 12:4–11; 1 Cor. 1:18–31.

AN ACTION TO TAKE: Our challenge is always to learn how to discern between self-interest and God's will. Faith invites us to seek and discern God's voice every day. Let's make this a daily discipline.

A PRAYER TO MAKE: 'Lord, develop my discernment skills so I can speak Your word with boldness and see wonders in Jesus' name. Amen.'

Waverley Abbey College

Education that changes lives

Our programmes equip students with the skills and knowledge to release their God-given potential to operate in roles that help people.

Central to all of our teaching is the Waverley Integrative Framework. Built on 50 years of experience, the model emphasises the importance of genuineness, unconditional acceptance and empathy in relationships. The courses we offer range from certificates to Higher Education level.

Counselling

As society begins to realise the extent of its brokenness, we continue to recognise the need to train people to support those who are struggling with everyday life, providing training to equip individuals to become professional counsellors. Whatever their starting point in academic learning, we have a pathway to help all students on their academic journey.

Spiritual Formation

For those wanting to be better equipped to help others on their spiritual journey, this programme provides robust and effective Spiritual Formation training. Students engage with theology, psychology, social sciences, historical studies, counselling, leadership studies and psychotherapy.

For more information about all of our course offerings available, visit **waverleyabbeycollege.ac.uk** or email **admissions@waverleyabbeycollege.ac.uk**

Stillness

Psalm 46

'He says, "Be still, and know that I am God; I will be exalted among the nations, I will be exalted in the earth."' (v10)

Leaving a powerful prayer meeting, we are returned to life's everyday reality. Living *Every Day with Jesus* invites us to develop the habit of finding God in our everyday experience. We can then testify to His ever present help when trouble engulfs us (Psa. 46:1–3).

My greatest battles are in my own mind. It will, unaided, conjure up all sorts of frightening scenarios. Such thoughts are real and intimidating. I can struggle to find the courage to confront them. They have the power to wake and rob me of my sleep; no time is quite as lonely as those wakeful, early morning hours.

Yet, the psalmist, considering life's horrors, declares these simple words, 'Be still and know'. The basis for such quiet confidence is the reality that God is with us; a fortress within whom we can take shelter.

When I wake in the early hours, feeling disconcerted and stressed, internally restless – almost breathless – I get up and go to my place of prayer. It's often a battle to focus on God, but slowly I do battle to take my stand in stillness and in calm. The battle is to be expected for the devil always wants to destabilise us, to intimidate us and place doubts in our head. Satan's first question is always, 'Has God said...?' The temptation is to be overwhelmed by, and begin to drown beneath, our situation; the challenge is to rest in the provision and protection of God as our fortress.

RELATED SCRIPTURE TO CONSIDER: Gen. 3:1–13; Psa. 18:1–6; 1 Cor. 2:10–16; 2 Cor. 4:1–12.

AN ACTION TO TAKE: Establish a regular place to pray and read Scripture in your home. By going there you will remind yourself that God is your fortress, 'an ever present help in trouble' (Psa. 46:1).

A PRAYER TO MAKE: 'Lord, when sleepless and distressed may I turn to prayer and learn to be still and know Your presence. Amen.'

Psalm 18:20–24
'For I have kept the ways of the LORD; I am not guilty of turning from my God.' (v21)

The great promise of Jesus is that the kingdom of God finds expression on earth. Christianity is not 'pie in the sky when you die', as some critics claim. For heaven broke into this world in the person of Jesus. Now risen and ascended to pray beside His Father for the world He came to save, we are invited to walk in His footsteps, guided by the Holy Spirit.

Watching a toddler learning to walk is a joy. Their will outruns their ability, but not their belief. They pull themselves up on anything available and launch into the unknown, staggering until gravity returns them to the floor. Seldom discouraged they repeat this exercise until they joyfully make their way into the celebratory arms of a beaming parent.

That's how I see my Christian life. I know the kingdom way and make consistent attempts to pull myself up and stagger in Jesus' footsteps. I tumble and fall frequently. Slowly I gain my walking skills and assume I've mastered walking, until I trip or fall. Most recently I was walking whilst gazing intently at something and walked straight into a lamppost, to which I instinctively apologised. Now I was the street spectacle!

God's ways invite us to develop a kingdom walk on earth. We may stumble and fall; we might injure ourselves or our pride. But we must always haul ourselves back up and keep going.

RELATED SCRIPTURE TO CONSIDER: Psa. 18:30–36; Luke 11:1–4; Rom. 12:1–3; Col. 1:3–14.

AN ACTION TO TAKE: Think about how steady you are on your feet. What are the trip hazards in your path as you walk the kingdom way?

A PRAYER TO MAKE: 'Lord, search me and see if there is any offensive way in me, and lead me into the kingdom way. Amen.' (See Psalm 139.)

2 Chronicles 6:3–15

'LORD, the God of Israel, there is no God like you in heaven or on earth – you who keep your covenant of love with your servants who continue wholeheartedly in your way.' (v14)

A covenant is a binding promise. Usually made between two parties, it places responsibilities on both parties. The covenant's benefits are dependent upon both parties keeping their covenant throughout its term. The word simply means to come together, and that is the work of Jesus. He has come and restored the family relationship with our creator.

When my father worked in the city of London, he said much business was done over lunch. A simple handshake was as solid an agreement as a carefully researched legal contract. A person's word was their bond. How far we have moved as a society in sixty years!

Yet, God takes us at our word. No contracts, instead a simple verbal promise. God makes His promise through His Word, Jesus. This is then recorded and revealed through God's living Word, Scripture. In every page we find God's wholehearted promise to humanity. We are invited to make our wholehearted response, committed beyond any doubt, to God.

Here's the challenge. God's covenant promises His presence and provision for all society yet requires that we agree to keep its terms completely. When we see God's influence diminishing throughout society it's not that God's 'batteries' are failing. It's a clear indication that we, God's people, are defaulting on our covenant commitment. Let's look this week at this covenant in detail.

RELATED SCRIPTURE TO CONSIDER: Deut. 29; Hos. 6:1–3; Matt. 26:26–29; Heb. 4:12–13.

AN ACTION TO TAKE: Think about how good you are at keeping your word. Read Scripture and take notes on the word God invites you to keep.

A PRAYER TO MAKE: 'Lord, let Your word that You have promised come true. Amen.'

2 Chronicles 6:16–18

'But will God really dwell on earth with humans? The heavens, even the highest heavens, cannot contain you. How much less this temple that I have built!' (v18)

For many, the very concept of God is unbelievable. It lies beyond our human capacity to understand. After all if it didn't, God would be reduced to the level of our understanding. Yet God remains, all powerful, all knowledgeable and present everywhere continuously.

Here, Solomon's prayer raises the question that was answered in Jesus. We are the beneficiaries of God's incarnate life and ministry in Him. Where once God was manifest in a mobile tabernacle, then a static temple, today that same incomparable, indefinable reality of God resides within those who choose to say yes to Jesus. We are now temples of the Holy Spirit, God's presence.

Our mortality contains the eternal presence of God, the presence that existed before the world was formed and will exist after it ceases to turn upon its axis. It's humbling and challenging in equal measure. As Solomon declared, such temples cannot contain the infinitude of God. Yet, they do carry within them God's reality.

Our challenge is in ensuring that through our lives the very glory of God is manifest. That we live as those who through prayer and service choose to ensure that God's order is realised on earth. This is our primary calling as God's servants. We are the points of presence that can call for revival both in our personal walk of faith and subsequently across our communities.

RELATED SCRIPTURE TO CONSIDER: Gen. 1:1–3; Exod. 40:33–38; 1 Cor. 6; John 1:1–18.

AN ACTION TO TAKE: Think about being God's mobile, mortal temple and the wonder of carrying God's glory within you. You carry His presence into every situation you find yourself in.

A PRAYER TO MAKE: 'Lord, from this mortal temple of mine let Your light shine out and reveal the life and light of Christ. Amen.'

2 Chronicles 6:19–21
'Yet, LORD my God, give attention to your servant's prayer and his plea for mercy. Hear the cry and the prayer that your servant is praying in your presence.' (v19)

Two questions come to mind when considering prayer. First, how can God personally engage with the individual prayers from all over the world, presented 24/7? The short answer is precisely because God is God. Some struggle with that response, indicating the limits to human understanding. If we assume human ingenuity will run this world effectively, then we must think again. Wilfully excluding God from life is to dismiss the creator, the one who can best assist in ordering life, from the micro to the macro.

Second, how is it that someone like me can become a temple for God's Spirit? That again is by God's grace. However, just as the Tabernacle and the Jerusalem Temple were subject to rules of holiness and required certain practices, so we are to consider how we are to live as such temples.

Every day we are to ask ourselves how we're carrying God's light. Do my words and actions give expression to that glory? What does my prayer life give birth to as I navigate the ups and downs of life?

Our constant prayer must be that we call out to God in intercession for the world around us, whilst carefully ensuring that everywhere we go, we remain a perpetual expression of the prayers our lips offer daily. We need joined up thinking; prayer and action are delicately interlinked.

RELATED SCRIPTURE TO CONSIDER: Josh. 1:1–9; Psa. 34; John 9:13–41; Philip. 4:4–13.

AN ACTION TO TAKE: At the start of each day remind yourself that you are a container of God's Holy Spirit. May your temple offer a daily witness to God's mercy, love and kindness.

A PRAYER TO MAKE: 'Lord, may every place I set my foot reflect the character of the God I worship. Amen.'

Relationships

2 Chronicles 6:22–23

'When anyone wrongs their neighbour and is required to take an oath and they come and swear the oath before your altar in this temple, then hear from heaven and act.' (vv22–23a)

Over the next six days we'll explore the six critical issues Solomon lay as the foundation stones on which the temple of the Holy Spirit stands. If a foundation stone falls into disrepair the stability of the whole structure is threatened. Our lives are to be established upon God's keystone, who is Jesus.

Relationships rightly lie at the heart of our Christian faith. A relationship originally lost through human action was restored, at great price, by Jesus. And God places such a high value on human relationships. Listening to people's stories, it's often the brutalising effects of poor relationships that rob them of joy, create bitter memories and produce poor mental health.

We're made in God's image (James 3:9) and can observe how everyone carries this image on their face. Passing people in the street I quietly pray for them. Their two eyes and nose form the sign of the cross and I choose to gaze upon each through the cross of Christ and pray.

We can't choose to withhold forgiveness; the one who owed humanity nothing extended forgiveness freely, despite our initial rejection, which impaled Jesus upon the cross. Again, if I pray the words Jesus taught in prayer, 'forgive us our offences as we forgive those who offend us', when I withhold forgiveness then I invite God to withhold forgiveness from me.

RELATED SCRIPTURE TO CONSIDER: Gen. 1:26–31; Isa. 28:16–19; Matt. 5:21–26; Eph. 2:11–22.

AN ACTION TO TAKE: It's time to reflect upon those fractured relationships. How you've been hurt and how you have hurt others. Going forward, bring these kinds of situations to God each day as they arise.

A PRAYER TO MAKE: 'Lord, I choose to forgive others because I am forever grateful You forgive me. Amen.'

2 Chronicles 6:24–25
**'Then hear from heaven and forgive the sin of your people
Israel and bring them back to the land you gave to them
and their ancestors.'** (v25)

'Enemy' often means an external, human threat and thoughts of
physical warfare. Yet, Scripture reminds us that our greatest
warfare is with sin. An unfashionable concept today, sin is
anything that leads us away from God. There's no value spectrum to
measure sin against – a minor indiscretion to a major crime. Sin is
simply everything, great and small, that obscures the risen Lord.

Confession is a critical foundation on which to build our walk of
faith. Rather than reacting to criticism, I can choose to recognise
much is true. I'm a fallen human who's only able to stand by God's
grace. We can't add an inch to our height, or an hour to our life. We're
completely dependent upon God.

Our promised land is living in God's immediate presence, yet we
easily stray back into the wilderness. The temptation to step away
from God is our greatest enemy. The mind is assaulted by unwelcome
thoughts that seek to steer us towards decisions beyond God's best.

I find this is my greatest contest. Resisting temptation's attempt to
control my life is the warfare I must engage in if I'm to abide in God's
provision. Here alone is my life exclusively available to God's purpose
to which I first surrendered. We are challenged when seeking to
live for righteousness in a world deceived by the swirling mists that
deceive so many seeking to realise their true potential.

RELATED SCRIPTURE TO CONSIDER: 2 Sam. 11; Psa. 141; Matt. 5:33–37;
Rom. 6:15–23.

AN ACTION TO TAKE: Deal with temptation by acknowledging it to yourself and
God, deliberately getting up and walking away from it (Gen. 39:11–12), and
if possible talk with a trusted Christian friend.

A PRAYER TO MAKE: 'Lord, give me the courage and conviction to flee from
temptation. Amen.'

2 Chronicles 6:26–31

'When famine or plague comes to the land, or blight or mildew, locusts or grasshoppers, or when enemies besiege them in any of their cities, whatever disaster or disease may come' (v28)

I grew up anticipating that through democratic government, the ills of the world would be addressed. Even after conversion, aged 19, I remained active in special interest initiatives. Today I find myself wondering if the energy I sincerely invested, and the resources I contributed, were the best use of my time.

There are without doubt inequalities across the globe as well as up and down the UK. I applaud the many compassionate initiatives in response to a vast ocean of global need. Yet, I find myself wondering if my time might not have been better spent in prayer. It is often said that we are in part the answer to our prayers. In fact God is the answer to all our prayers. On occasion God may choose to work through us as vehicles of His grace. Constructive initiatives run the danger of tempting us toward pride in our endeavours.

This is not to say that our participation in life, in employment and within our communities is not an opportunity to demonstrate the reality of God. But this is surely the natural outworking of being a disciple of Jesus. It is through prayer that God has promised to work within His creation. My most profitable investment as a Christian is to pray. It's the one reason it is so keenly contested by the devil and for so many years, to my shame, it occupied so little of my time.

RELATED SCRIPTURE TO CONSIDER: Eccl. 9:7–18; Psa. 84; Mark 9:1–29; Eph. 6:18–20.

AN ACTION TO TAKE: I'd recommend two resources. The first is *Pathway into Prayer*, a free booklet available to download from **waverleyabbeyresources.org**. The other a free book by A. W. Tozer, *The Praying Plumber* from **edwj.org/mj21-19jun**

A PRAYER TO MAKE: 'Lord, may my actions never take me away from my daily time of prayer. Amen.'

2 Chronicles 6:32–33

Do whatever the foreigner asks of you, so that all the peoples of the earth may know your name and fear you, as do your own people Israel. (v33)

In times of hardship it's easy to look for a scapegoat; someone on whom we can lay the blame for our misdeeds. That's the Old Testament role of the scapegoat. All too often we look for someone who looks and behaves differently. Throughout history this has led to the oppression of people on the basis of their ethnicity.

Given we are all made in God's image, we have no right to distinguish someone on grounds of race. Indeed in Christ there is no difference recognised between races. More challenging perhaps is the fact that God invites prayer from everyone, be they disciple or not.

In lockdown my own daughter experienced this. Her income stopped overnight. She wasn't entitled to benefits. She rang and said, 'Dad, what can I do?' I said, 'You may not like the answer, but I suggest you pray'. 'Does it matter that I'm not sure if I believe all you do about God?' 'No. God just wants you to start praying. God will direct the outcomes.' She phoned a week later. She discerned specific answers to her prayers. Her interest and confidence in God began to grow.

We're not to blame the 'foreigner', or 'the other'. We are to welcome and pray that their practical needs are met, and that they find Christ. We have no need to blame anyone for the state of our world. It's the consequence of sin. Our response is to pray, to love and to serve.

RELATED SCRIPTURE TO CONSIDER: Lev. 16:6–22; 2 Kings 5; Luke 7:1–10; Gal. 3:26–29.

AN ACTION TO TAKE: Take time to acknowledge where you are prejudiced. Bring such prejudices to God and ask Him to ensure they do not misdirect your prayers or determine your actions.

A PRAYER TO MAKE: 'Lord, help me to pray for the many 'others' who live among me. Meet their needs and lead them to Christ. Amen.'

2 Chronicles 6:34–35
'then hear from heaven their prayer and their plea, and uphold their cause.' (v35)

Prayer presents a challenge and a mystery to all. It's easy to feel discouraged with prayer. In prayer we engage in warfare in God's name, and war disrupts all of life. God's promises are always fiercely contested and we're invited to enrol in the battle and to make God's cause our cause.

Effective prayer demands regular practice. It is the road along which God's grace flows, always up against Satan's armed resistance. Every time we pray we go to war. In war-torn Bosnia in the early nineties I visited Christian communities, an unforgettable and frightening experience. One church community, who, at great risk, were shielding Christian Serbs and Croats, gathered to pray. Indeed prayer was their primary occupation as bullets and shells were exchanged across a frontline not one mile away. A reminder that war is about confronting and defeating the reality of evil itself.

Today, prayer is the cause God has asked me to take up with my life. In the months ahead Waverley Abbey Trust will establish a circle of prayer around the UK, and in partnership with 24–7 Prayer, already with an established community in Waverley Abbey House. Together we will engage in unceasing prayer to see God move afresh in these lands.

RELATED SCRIPTURE TO CONSIDER: Psa. 130; 1 Kings 18:16–45; Matt. 26:36–46; Mark 13:1–13.

AN ACTION TO TAKE: You will have causes in your life. Is it time to promote prayer and make God's cause your cause?

A PRAYER TO MAKE: 'Lord, You are my God. Increase my hunger and thirst for Your will to be done on earth and to turn to You in prayer more often. Amen.'

Forgive Us

2 Chronicles 6:36–39

'Then from heaven, your dwelling-place, hear their prayer and their pleas, and uphold their cause. And forgive your people, who have sinned against you.' (v39)

Forgiveness turns the world right side up. God has always known this, and demonstrated the power of forgiveness through the life and death of Jesus. The undeserving, including us, were offered an opportunity to renew friendship with their creator.

At a more mundane level, forgiveness has been scientifically shown to improve our health. A recent professional journal carried the headline, 'How stress degrades and forgiveness protects health.'[1] It suggests that 'developing a more forgiving coping style may help minimize stress-related disorders'.

The cross rises above history as a prayer of forgiveness for all time. Its victim, Jesus, now resurrected and ascended, makes intercession beside the Father for fallen humanity. We join our prayers with His, and know that the greatest gift we offer to the world is the reconciliation between humanity and God. For as forgiveness is received, a new citizen, a sinner rescued from sin and destruction, is born. A citizen who embraces the act of forgiveness as a way of life and seeks to live every day with Jesus in loving God and neighbour.

Forgiveness lies at the heart of all prayer. Both in our own forgiveness and then asking God to intervene and bring people to repentance and faith. There may be many complex mechanisms for managing human relationships, but everyone longs to enjoy the freedom of knowing they are forgiven, accepted and loved.

[1] https://journals.sagepub.com/doi/abs/10.1177/1359105314544132 (Accessed January 2021)

RELATED SCRIPTURE TO CONSIDER: Psa. 103; Micah 7:8–20; Luke 7:36–50; Eph. 3:14–21.

AN ACTION TO TAKE: Finding forgiveness is wonderful, but knowing you're forgiven transforms your life. In what ways are you free to love and forgive others because of God's loving acceptance?

A PRAYER TO MAKE: 'Lord, show compassion to those ruled by the hatred born of hurt and misunderstanding. I pray that as I am forgiven I will forgive others. Amen.'

2 Chronicles 6:40–42

'Now, my God, may your eyes be open and your ears attentive to the prayers offered in this place.' (v40)

Solomon draws his prayer of dedication of the Temple to a close. We have identified six foundation stones upon which God's temple is established. These are: right relationships, refusing to sin, trusting in God's provision, offering everyone the love of God, engaging in spiritual warfare, and knowing that true freedom is the fruit of forgiveness.

These are the qualities of God's kingdom on earth, for which we both pray and work. God is constantly scanning the world for those who make a sincere commitment to build their lives upon these six foundation stones. We are established as temples of the Holy Spirit who consistently reveal the life of God and point the way to salvation in Christ Jesus.

We do this not out of a sense of duty, nor to reinforce a theological truth. No! We do it out of a deepening friendship with God. Amazingly Jesus Himself calls us His friends (John 15:15), if we obey all that He tells us. The Temple, like the Tabernacle that preceded it, had at its heart the Holy of Holies. Only the High Priest might enter, and then only once a year. When Jesus died on the cross, the curtain that separated the Holy of Holies was torn and everyone choosing faith in Jesus is now invited into the very presence of God.

The prayers we make are an offering to God, requests that God's will is done on earth. The sacrifice pleasing to God is a broken and contrite heart.

RELATED SCRIPTURE TO CONSIDER: Lev. 16:1–17; Psa. 51; John 14:15–27; John 5:9–15.

AN ACTION TO TAKE: We carry the life of God within us everywhere we go. God sees all we do and hears all we say. Consider: are you happy with the offerings of the deeds and words you present to God?

A PRAYER TO MAKE: 'Lord, please receive my sacrifice – a broken spirit and a broken and contrite heart. Amen.' (See Psalm 51:17.)

Fire

2 Chronicles 7:1–6

'When Solomon finished praying, fire came down from heaven and consumed the burnt offering and the sacrifices, and the glory of the Lord filled the temple.' (v1)

On Pentecost Sunday we noted how the disciples, gathered in the Upper Room, 'saw what seemed to be tongues of fire' come and rest on each of them. This after nine days of prayer, from Christ's Ascension until Pentecost. God answered their prayer with His presence. It is indeed the presence of God that we seek through prayer; God present with us and God's presence in response to the subject of our prayers.

There is a danger that we can, perhaps unintentionally, domesticate God. Out of commitment and love we only invite God to operate within the boundaries which we feel comfortable. Yet, fire can spread very quickly and is not something that naturally submits to human rules.

We've seen the immense bushfires across Australia that, in an instant, consume peoples' homes and livelihoods. They move unpredictably and resist attempts to dowse them. Fire has also proved essential in human development. Today it keeps us warm and has the capacity to change the composition of those things it touches, for both positive and negative outcomes.

It is not an element we are to treat lightly, for its power can prove irresistible. That's why it's a metaphor for God – a consuming fire (Heb. 12:29). It is clear that to take God seriously quite literally means to work with fire, yet this is the reality of God's presence; He's not someone to be taken lightly.

RELATED SCRIPTURE TO CONSIDER: Exod. 13:17–22; Deut. 4:15–31; Rom. 12:1–3; Heb. 10:19–36.

AN ACTION TO TAKE: Consider if there are limits beyond which you would find it uncomfortable trusting in God.

A PRAYER TO MAKE: 'Lord, let me remain upon Your altar as a living sacrifice, and may my life always be acceptable in Your sight. Amen.'

Ambassadors of Hope

The Bible reveals that as Christians our citizenship is in heaven (Phil. 3:20). Yet, Paul recognised that many live as 'enemies of the cross'. As heavenly citizens we have a responsibility to represent the interests and values of God's kingdom here on earth. But how might that be done?

In the next issue we will together explore how God instructs and enables us to live as ambassadors of hope within a secular age.

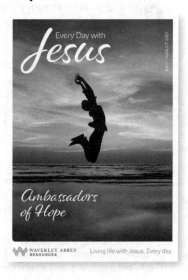

Also available as esubscription, ebook, audioversion and PDF.

2 Chronicles 7:11–18

'if my people, who are called by my name, will humble themselves and pray and seek my face and turn from their wicked ways, then I will hear from heaven, and I will forgive their sin and will heal their land.' (v14)

God instructs us to turn to prayer when things are difficult. In an increasingly self-centred society, it's easy only to think of my difficulties. Yet, I have died with Christ, and I no longer live, but rather Christ lives in me. The real difficulty is the state of our world.

There are huge problems from pandemics to famine, and we're foolish to assume that political will can resolve such issues. Prayer alone offers a means by which we can call out to God on behalf of our world. This lies well beyond our imagination, for imagination seeks to comprehend a reality, the edges of which can only be touched – much as the haemorrhaging woman was able to touch the hem of Jesus' garment (Mark 5:25–34).

There is humility required to acknowledge that the needs of our world cannot be met by our educated sophistication.

Prayer is also inauthentic if we are two-faced as we pray – one face turned toward God, the other only concerned for our own welfare. It was Selwyn Hughes' who said, 'whatever part God plays in spiritual awakening, we have a part to play too'.

Great doors swing on small hinges. The hinge is a life devoted to God and invested in humble prayer. Revival requires prayer.

RELATED SCRIPTURE TO CONSIDER: Isa. 1:15–20; Matt. 9:20–22; Rom. 6:1–14; Gal. 2:19–21.

AN ACTION TO TAKE: Following our conversion we are cleansed of sin, as shown through baptism. Sadly, as we journey through life, we get dirty. We don't need a fresh baptism, but we do need to repent and decide how far we want to pursue God.

A PRAYER TO MAKE: 'Lord, help me to see by faith that through authentic prayer I can contribute to Your work throughout the world. Amen.'

2 Chronicles 7:19–22

'This temple will become a heap of rubble. All who pass by will be appalled and say, "Why has the Lord done such a thing to this land and to this temple?"' (v21)

I n a tolerant society, disagreement is too quickly characterised as bigotry. Whilst we pride ourselves on the value of free speech, political correctness can dumb down public discourse. This presents a real and present danger for Christianity today.

Yet, as Christians, living as temples of the Holy Spirit, God requires obedience to His Word. It appears to be easier accommodating social and cultural norms than articulating areas of profound disagreement. But knowledge is always a product of diverse views engaging in open, honest, if robust, conversation. Conversation that is not biased by social media or special interest groups.

The greatest danger to true freedom is always when we fail to speak up about what we believe and why. Anyone engaged in public discourse can neither demand to control the public discourse, nor insist on the exclusion of another's voice on the basis of their preconceived understanding. God warns us that we are to live God's way in God's world, and that includes how we act in public discourse. And global scepticism that all news is 'fake news' threatens to destroy the very foundation, free speech, upon which such a free society is established.

One reason revival waits is because we have lost our confidence in God and our competence to live by God's promise alone. Is my temple anything more than rubble?

RELATED SCRIPTURE TO CONSIDER: Psa. 127; Dan. 3; Matt. 10:16–20; Acts 24:9–26.

AN ACTION TO TAKE: Prayer is expressed through our words and through our lives. Are we strong as God's temples and making the case for the good news?

A PRAYER TO MAKE: 'Lord, I want to live my life as a clear statement that our God reigns. Help me continually to maintain this temple of the Holy Spirit. Amen.'

Numbers 24:1–14

'Even if Balak gave me all the silver and gold in his palace, I could not do anything of my own accord, good or bad, to go beyond the command of the LORD – and I must say only what the LORD says.' (v13)

The story of Balaam is normally remembered because his donkey spoke. However, it's really a story of speaking truth to power. Balaam had to choose between God and himself. King Balak promised him great rewards if he did as he was ordered. Indeed, it appears Balaam had a reputation for divination, seeking knowledge about the future by supernatural means, something condemned by God who alone holds the future in His hands.

God always invites us to consider our long-term happiness; sin entices us with immediate, apparent, satisfaction. God intends to establish consistency in our life and witness through obedience. Balaam had his pride dented when God needed to speak to him through his donkey. But this was an act of God's love, a reminder to open his eyes and remain true to God's word.

Our great challenge is to become increasingly sensitive to how God invites us to live our lives. In the face of opportunity are we able to discern His voice and obey His direction? Where our heart is willing, He will place prompts along our path to remind and encourage us in His direction.

RELATED SCRIPTURE TO CONSIDER: Num. 22:20–35; Josh. 5:2–9; Luke 19:28–40; John 14:15–21.

AN ACTION TO TAKE: Life demands that we take decisions. Those decisions, and the fruit from them, will reveal who we obey. Does your decision making include God? Our reward may not be immediate contentment.

A PRAYER TO MAKE: 'Lord, I want to hear and obey Your voice and take my stand on the truth of Your Word. Amen.'

Keep Going

1 Thessalonians 5:12–24

'Rejoice always, pray continually, give thanks in all circumstances; for this is God's will for you in Christ Jesus.' (vv16–18)

It can be assumed that living and serving God is restrictive given the open nature of today's society. Whilst we cannot determine the direction within which society moves, we can take responsibility in the degree to which we will swim with the tide.

My own experience in building my relationship with God is that I have made some poor decisions along the way. My words and actions have hurt others in my attempts to protect myself. This I imagine is true for all of those who have embraced the challenge of living every day with Jesus.

Scripture is clear: the human heart is instinctively wicked. No matter how I wrestle with it, I cannot correct its drift towards wrongdoing. However, we have only to submit to God in humble acceptance that without Him we can do nothing.

But with God we are invited to live by a clear set of values and practices. Learning to rejoice and give thanks in all circumstances is tough when circumstances are not what we anticipated or desired. Yet, it is God's challenge to each of us to first find Him where we are. This requires prayer and yields a tremendous fruit. For the greatest evidence to the love of God is a life lived in celebration of His promise and purpose.

It takes courage born of faith in the promise of God to live the Christian life. It is that faith we are to nurture each day, which we can only do as we deliberately take time with Jesus every day.

RELATED SCRIPTURE TO CONSIDER: Psa. 40:1–5; Jer. 17:5–10; Col. 3:1–4; James 4:6–12.

AN ACTION TO TAKE: Consider what prevents you from spending time daily with God and living the life of a disciple as described in the Bible.

A PRAYER TO MAKE: 'Lord, help me to rejoice always, pray continually, and give thanks in all circumstances. Amen.'

Prayer

Psalm 51

'Have mercy on me, O God, according to your unfailing love, according to your great compassion blot out my transgressions.' (v1)

As we conclude our journey looking at the seeds for revival, there are three essential strands that emerge which Scripture commands us to practice. The first essential is prayer.

Such prayer has two core components and these are clearly expressed in King David's great prayer. They are repentance and request. Every time we approach God, make confession and repent, within moments we stand in need of forgiveness again. Our lives are characterised by the fracture of sinfulness. Whilst our standing with God is changed the instant we surrender our lives to Jesus, the shadow of our corruption continues to accompany us through life.

Perhaps the greatest sin of all is human pride, which attempts to hold its own before God. Pride is always our attempt to draw attention to ourselves and our accomplishments, when we could learn from the Holy Spirit, Who only and always points to Jesus. Repentance is the prayer that recognises our total dependence upon God. Without God I have nothing and I am nobody.

Once I recognise that all things hold together in God alone, then I recognise that there is only one influential and reliable source to whom I can make my requests. If we are serious about seeing God revive His people and this nation then our prayer must be committed, consistent and compassionate.

RELATED SCRIPTURE TO CONSIDER: Hab. 3:2 & 16–18; Luke 11:5–12; Philip. 4:4–9; Col. 1:15–23.

AN ACTION TO TAKE: Make a plan for yourself that ensures you are consistent, committed and compassionate in prayer.

A PRAYER TO MAKE: 'Lord, have mercy on me. May my eyes be focussed on You as I pray Your will be done on earth. Amen.'

James 1:22–27

'But whoever looks intently into the perfect law that gives freedom and continues in it – not forgetting what they have heard but doing it – they will be blessed in what they do.' (v25)

The second essential strand Scripture demands of us is obedience. This impacts our thoughts, our words and our deeds. I often end my day by making a prayerful reflection inviting God to bring to mind the thoughts, words and deeds that were unnecessary. They may have been unkind, untrue and more about massaging my pride through criticising others than about appealing to God for mercy and help.

It is one thing to lay claim to the promises of Christ, quite another to submit one's life ruthlessly to be shaped by them. I enjoy gardening and I have discovered that rich harvests require radical pruning. Jesus made this clear to His disciples. Little wonder then, that so much of 'me' requires pruning so there's an opportunity for God's blossom to form kingdom fruit. And as with every fruit-bearing tree, their harvest is never for themselves but the nourishment of others.

God looks to see that our lives are an open expression of His will revealed through His Word. Active attention to obedience is essential. We receive the basic toolkit, the fruit of the Spirit, the moment we choose Christ. The Christian disciple's due diligence is regularly to audit behaviour to ensure that our faith determines both our feelings and our actions. Learning to live God's way is a disciplined process, and one we do well to talk through with fellow committed disciples.

RELATED SCRIPTURE TO CONSIDER: Exod. 20:1–21; Isa. 58; John 15:1–8; Gal. 5:13–26.

AN ACTION TO TAKE: Consider how the fruit of the Spirit practically shapes your feelings and behaviour.

A PRAYER TO MAKE: 'Lord, help me to live my life aligned with Your chosen path as revealed throughout Scripture. Amen.'

Notes

Order form

Get Your **FREE** Daily Bible Reading Notes **TODAY!** (UK ONLY)

Your favourite Bible Reading notes are now available to you for FREE. God has called us back to the original vision of CWR to provide these notes to everyone who needs them, regardless of their circumstance or ability to pay. It is our desire to see these daily Bible reading notes used more widely, to see Christians grow in their relationship with Jesus on a daily basis and to see Him reflected in their everyday living. Clearly there are costs to provide this ministry and we are trusting in God's provision.

Could you be part of this vision? Do you have the desire to see lives transformed through a relationship with Jesus? **A small donation from you of just £2 a month, by direct debit, will make such a difference** Giving hope to someone in desperate need whilst you too grow deeper in your own relationship with Jesus.

4 Easy Ways To Order

1. Visit our online store at **waverleyabbeyresources.org/store**
2. Send this form together with your payment to:
   CWR, Waverley Abbey House, Waverley Lane, Farnham, Surrey GU9 8EP
3. Phone in your credit card order: **01252 784700** (Mon–Fri, 9.30am – 4.30pm)
4. Visit a Christian bookshop

For a list of our National Distributors, who supply countries outside the UK, visit waverleyabbeyresources.org/distributors

Your Details (required for orders and donations)

Full Name:	CWR ID No. (if known):
Home Address:	
	Postcode:
Telephone No. (for queries):	Email:

Publications

TITLE	QTY	PRICE	TOTAL
	Total Publications		

UK P&P: up to £24.99 = **£2.99**; £25.00 and over = **FREE**

Elsewhere P&P: up to £10 = **£4.95**; £10.01 – £50 = **£6.95**; £50.01 – £99.99 = **£10**; £100 and over = **£30**

Total Publications and P&P (please allow 14 days for delivery)	**A**	

Payment Details

☐ I enclose a cheque made payable to CWR for the amount of: **£** _____

☐ Please charge my credit/debit card.

Cardholder's Name (in BLOCK CAPITALS) _____

Card No. ☐☐☐☐ ☐☐☐☐ ☐☐☐☐ ☐☐☐☐ ☐☐☐☐

Expires End ☐☐ ☐☐   Security Code ☐☐☐

Continued overleaf >>

One off Special Gift to CWR ☐ Please send me an acknowledgement of my gift **B** [ ]

GRAND TOTAL (Total of A & B) [ ]

Gift Aid (your home address required, see overleaf)

giftaid it I am a UK taxpayer and want CWR to reclaim the tax on all my donations for the four years prior to this year **and on** all donations I make from the date of this Gift Aid declaration until further notice.*

Taxpayer's Full Name (in BLOCK CAPITALS) _____

Signature _____ **Date** _____

*I am a UK taxpayer and understand that if I pay less Income Tax and/or Capital Gains Tax than the amount of Gift Aid claimed on all my donations in that ta year it is my responsibility to pay any difference.

Your FREE Daily Bible Reading Notes Order

	Please Tick	FREE	£2 pcm	£5 pcm	£10 pcm	Other
Every Day with Jesus (1yr, 6 issues)		☐	☐	☐	☐	☐ £ ___
Large Print *Every Day with Jesus* (1yr, 6 issues)		☐	☐	☐	☐	☐ £ ___
Inspiring Women Every Day (1yr, 6 issues)		☐	☐	☐	☐	☐ £ ___

All CWR Bible reading notes are also available in single issue **ebook** and **email subscription** format. Visit **waverleyabbeyresources.org** for further info

CWR Instruction to your Bank or Building Society to pay by Direct Debit

DIREC Debi

Please fill in the form and send to to: CWR, Waverley Abbey House, Waverley Lane, Farnham, Surrey GU9 8EP

Name and full postal address of your Bank or Building Society

To: The Manager   Bank/Building Society

Address

Postcode

Name(s) of Account Holder(s)

Branch Sort Code

Bank/Building Society Account Number

Originator's Identification Number

4	2	0	4	8	7

Reference

Instruction to your Bank or Building Society

Please pay CWR Direct Debits from the account detailed in this Instru subject to the safeguards assured by the Direct Debit Guarantee. I understand that this Instruction may remain with CWR and, if so, deta will be passed electronically to my Bank/Building Society.

Signature(s)

Date

Banks and Building Societies may not accept Direct Debit Instructions for some types of account

For a subscription outside of the UK please visit www.waverleyabbeyresources.or where you will find a list of our national distributors.

How would you like to hear from us? We would love to keep you up to date on all aspects of the CWR ministry, including; new publications, events & courses as well as how you can support us.

If you **DO** want to hear from us on email, please tick here [ ] If you **DO NOT** want us to contact you by post, please tick her You can update your preferences at any time by contacting our customer services team on 01252 784 700. You can view our privacy policy online at waverleyabbeyresources.org